Hooligan

A Mormon Boyhood

Hooligan

A Mormon Boyhood

A memoir by Douglas Thayer

ZARAHEMLA BOOKS
Provo, Utah

© 2007 by Douglas Thayer

ISBN-13 978-0-9787971-5-7
ISBN-10 0-9787971-5-9

Cover design by Jason Robinson

Published by
Zarahemla Books
869 East 2680 North
Provo, UT 84604
info@zarahemlabooks.com
ZarahemlaBooks.com

To Marcus, Benson, Aaron, Jacob, William,
Heather, Lilian, Abigail, Maxwell, Anna,
and all the rest who inevitably will follow

1

square blocks, pie lady, Babylon, sin, Heber Creeper

A SLEEPY MORMON TOWN of fourteen or fifteen thousand, Provo was a splendid place to grow up for my friends and me. Our lives were mostly unattended once we were out of the house, but still governed by the four seasons, school, geography, Mormonism, and family. Yet we were not aware of these intrusions. Nobody seemed to worry about us boys much, as if perhaps we weren't of great value.

We were to be seen and not heard. Nobody was likely to steal one of us, and there were too few cars for there to be much danger of being run down, although we might die of polio or perhaps diphtheria, whooping cough, or gunshot, which took my friend Owen Hodson when he was twelve and classmate Reese Johnson at the same age.

The expression "to be taken," which my mother used on occasion, always bothered me growing up. I couldn't figure out who was taking him and where he was being taken and if he wanted to go, which I doubted, though perhaps it was something only faithful adult members of the church understood.

It was important to be faithful. In 1920 my grandparents, Frederick and Nora Thatcher, and my mother Lily and nine other children, like so many other faithful

Mormon converts, had heeded the call to leave Babylon and gather to the safe mountain valleys of Zion. Uncle T. Harry Heal, my grandmother's brother, had come to Provo in 1906, to be followed by his brother James; his four sisters, Emma, Emily, Nora, and Laura; and finally their parents, my Great-grandfather and Great-grandmother Heal. Uncle Harry's sister Henrietta had heeded the call to Zion earlier.

Settled in 1849 by pioneers, Provo was one of the towns south of Salt Lake City established by the Mormon prophet and colonizer Brigham Young. Ten or fifteen miles stretched between each town, Highway 89 connecting them all—Lehi, American Fork, Pleasant Grove, Lindon, Orem, Provo, Springville, Spanish Fork, Payson, and Salem. The towns hugged the Wasatch Mountains because of the rivers and streams flowing out of the deep canyons. Water was essential for towns and the irrigated farms. Without water there was no life in a largely arid state seared by the desert sun.

Canals coming off the Provo River provided water for the Utah County farms and town vegetable gardens. Connected by an intricate system of feeder ditches and gutters, the water flowed into the backyards. A family had its watering turn each week, which had to be strictly kept or the garden perished, unless it could be saved that one week with water from the hose or perhaps an artesian well.

Sometimes there were arguments and even fights over water turns, some neighbor or perhaps someone five or six blocks up the street taking the water too soon or releasing it too late. We heard that out on the farms, where water was crucial to the survival of crops, killings sometimes happened because of water, a farmer's skull crushed with a shovel because he was a water thief, perhaps the worst of all thieves.

One morning, as a boy of five, I came around the

corner of Mrs. Aird's house, where we had an apartment, to see my father standing on the front porch holding a long butcher knife and threatening the life of a neighbor, who stood holding a big rock and equally threatening my father's life. Apparently there had been some misuse of irrigation water. Both men cursed each other splendidly, but there was no murder committed that day, no red blood spilt on the sidewalk or Mrs. Aird's porch.

Mrs. Aird's was the first house of four in which we would live in the Sixth Ward, two before my mother divorced my father and two after. Mrs. Aird, a short, thin woman, rode a black bicycle and wore black clothes. I thought her a witch and fully expected to see her flying through the air on her bicycle some late night silhouetted against a full moon, when the bats came out, as they typically did. But I never saw this happen, which I regretted somewhat, although I was not as capable of regret at five or six as I would be later.

Provo, the county seat and shopping mecca for the whole valley, had grown and prospered, particularly during the First World War and the ten years after, but then the Depression came, and everything slowed down. Nothing seemed to change, and it wouldn't until the beginning of the Second World War in 1939 and the coming of the Geneva Steel Plant and the ten thousand construction workers it would take to build it on the shores of Utah Lake, out of the range of Japanese bombers. Before that, there were few if any new houses or buildings going up, no new businesses or jobs, no people moving in or out, the neighborhoods static.

Like other early Mormon towns, Provo was laid out in square blocks with sidewalks and wide tree-lined streets, many still unpaved and providing a supply of ammunition for rock fights. University Avenue ran north-south and Center Street east-west, cutting Provo into four main sections, each with its schools. The kids in our section, the southwest, perhaps the poorest of the four, all went to Franklin Elementary School, Dixon Junior High School, and then on to Provo High School with all the rest of the Provo kids. Except for an occasional farm, the foothills east of town were bare of houses and buildings. There was little traffic, with stop signs and stoplights necessary only on the most strategic corners and intersections.

The Mormons in Provo were divided into congregations by geographical divisions called wards—First, Second, Third, Fourth, Fifth, and Sixth Wards, and so on, all the wards part of the Utah Stake, the only Provo stake. The stake met every three months in the Provo Tabernacle in stake conference to hear the prophet and the apostles come down from Salt Lake to preach against sin and remind us all of the great sacrifices of the pioneers who came to Utah and the valleys of the mountains to establish Zion.

All church members were brothers and sisters in the gospel, which is what you called each other even if you weren't really brother or sister. And we boys identified ourselves in part by the ward we lived in. Each ward had its own chapel and often its own grocery store, which might be known by the name of the ward although the ward did not own it.

The Sixth Ward, where I and all my friends lived and—if we managed to stay on the straight and narrow path—attended Primary, Sunday School, priesthood meeting, and sacrament meeting, ran from University Avenue to Fifth West and from Center Street to the railroad yards and beyond. It was a big ward, a splendid place for roaming boys, its geographical area covering about thirty square blocks, if you didn't count the fields and Mud Lake sloughs south of the railroad tracks.

Highway 89, the state's lifeline, cut through the Sixth Ward's center on Third South.

It was the ward my Grandfather and Grandmother Thatcher had moved into when they made their 1920 exit from England. Granduncle Harry lived in the Sixth Ward, as did Grandaunt Emily. My mother's brothers, Uncles Harold and Leonard, and her sister, Aunt Doris, lived there. It was our family ward.

Great-grandfather Heal and his family had converted to Mormonism in Bath, England. The family story said that when the Mormon missionaries knocked on his door, he said, "Come in, my sons, I have waited long for thee." A religious man of great faith who sought the truth, he had seen the missionaries in a dream, and so he accepted their message of salvation and exaltation as revealed to the Mormon Prophet Joseph Smith. Although the Heals were not pioneers and hadn't been driven out of the Mormon city of Nauvoo, Illinois, in winter by the mobs bent on their destruction, hadn't died of cholera and fever, hadn't crossed the plains in wagons and handcarts, hadn't starved or frozen or been attacked by Indians, hadn't left new graves marking their path, still they were part of the gathering, acceptable Saints coming after the original pioneer era had ended.

None of my father's family lived in the Sixth Ward. In fact, I never met any of his family, not even a distant cousin. Born in 1865, he was thirty-five years older than my mother, came from California as far as we knew, and was not a member of the only true church.

The postman, iceman, coalman, and milkman were a part of Sixth Ward daily life, a chip of ice out of the horse-drawn ice wagon a boy's free summer treat, that and the soft sun-heated tar we dug up from the cracks in the road for gum, the embedded gravel keeping our teeth sharp. The pie lady pushed her converted baby buggy loaded with fresh homemade pies down the sidewalk calling, "Pies! Pies! Pies for supper!" A herd of milk cows came up Second West every morning on their way to pasture north of town by the brickyard and returned every evening, each cow turning voluntarily down its own lane. Twice daily the Heber Creeper, a small steam engine pulling its few cars, traveled the Denver and Rio Grande spur line up Second West to Provo Canyon and Heber Valley beyond.

During the Depression, Sixth Ward members were content if they could put food on the table, clothes on their backs, shoes on their feet, and a roof over their heads. We boys were often reminded in these hard times that we weren't living in the lap of luxury. We knew what a lap was but had no acquaintance with luxury, so we couldn't quite figure out what was meant. Our parents and other adults seemed to spend a great deal of time reminding us of things. We seemed to need a lot of reminding. We were frequently told that our heads were like sieves and that what we were told went in one ear and out the other.

In the late thirties, the possibility of glorious war was the only thing beyond the town and valley that interested boys. We also longed to become sixteen and finally eligible for our deer and driver's licenses, tokens of our beginning passage into manhood, our interest in girls but a dim shadow still undiscovered in our boys' bodies and minds.

2

Zion, WPA, harlot, police station, Sears, BB guns

Provo's business district up and down Center Street formed the north boundary of the Sixth Ward, so it was easily accessible afoot or on bikes and was a place of great interest for us boys. The district ran along both sides of Center Street from First East to Fifth West and Pioneer Park, with blocks and half-blocks running north and south. Summers we were often in town, digging through trash bins, roving through Kress's and Woolworth's, the five-and-dime stores whose wares we could sometimes afford. We visited weekly Carlson's, Stephen Bee's, Guessford's, and Sears, the best stores for sporting goods, where we bought our Red Ryder BB guns, BBs, and fishing stuff and later, when we were older, our .22s, shotguns, and deer rifles. We stopped to look into smoky, dimly lit pool halls and watched secretive men coming out of the state liquor store, keeping our eyes peeled, which boys were told to do. We picked up things from the counters and display cases, felt them, valuable things—bags of marbles, pocket knives, hunting knives, Big Little Books, heavy boxes of ammunition, fishing reels, and wrist watches.

Sears was the best for stealing pocket knives, if that's what a boy liked to do or found necessary, which I, early given to being good and later to being an ardent

Boy Scout, never did, thus limiting my earthly pleasures. Envious, filled with desire, we stood looking at the racks of shining guns behind the counters and the pistols safely under glass and out of reach. We knew all the brands—Parkers, Stevens, Ithicas, Brownings, Winchesters, Remingtons—desired to hold the guns, touch the cool blued metal, the warm polished wood, work the smooth actions. But we knew we had no right to ask because, young and without adequate wealth, we were not legitimate customers.

From the Center Street business district, the whole town and mountain valley, a paradise for roaming Sixth Ward boys, spread before us.

On the corner of University Avenue and Center Street was the Utah Stake tabernacle built by the pioneers, and next to that the Orem interurban station, and across University Avenue the white classic Greek-looking city and county building, and on the corner the city building with the police station in the basement. We boys heard stories about older boys arrested, handcuffed, being dragged down those stairs to their imprisonment and doom.

Straight east on Center Street ten or twelve blocks past Veterans Memorial Park was the Utah State Mental Hospital, one big white building facing toward town, the high mountains looming behind it. If we rode our bikes fast when we went up there and didn't stop, the crazy people couldn't catch us, drag us into the buildings or thick shrubs, and murder us. Back in the days when the spoils were being divided, Salt Lake got the prison, Ogden the reform school, and Provo the mental hospital.

North from Center Street up University Avenue five blocks was the Brigham Young University lower campus and beyond that on Temple Hill the upper campus. Farther out was the brick yard, the millrace, farms and orchards, and the Provo River where we swam naked and free. Across the river and up on the bench was Orem, with its thin two-mile-long business district and its vast apple, peach, cherry, and pear orchards, where a boy could work his fingers to the bone picking cherries at three cents a pound, peaches, apples, and pears yet too heavy for us to carry in the big canvas picking bags.

Farther west from Provo were fields and then Utah Lake, into which all the valley towns dumped their untreated sewage, the lake a great place for swimming, killing carp, creating sand cities, and building log rafts to float away on, never to return. Coming back east toward Provo, at the south boundary of the Sixth Ward were the Union Pacific railroad yards and hobo jungles. Further southeast lay the CCC Camp, Central Utah Vocational School, railroad roundhouse, golf course, county fairgrounds, and Provo airport. At night, safe in our beds but not asleep, or waking briefly, we Sixth Ward boys heard the far-off mournful train whistle inviting us to distant places and adventures and warning us that our boyhoods could not last forever.

We knew that the Heber Creeper whistle woke up sleeping ward members at five in the morning, which, we were told, was the reason there were so many kids in the Sixth Ward, but we didn't understand that reasoning. Tobe, Russell Madsen's dog, always howled in the late afternoon when the Creeper, blowing its whistle, came back down Second West on its return journey.

South of the Sixth Ward was Mud Lake, an arm of Utah Lake, and the sloughs. Farther south sat Springville, the next town, and before that the Ironton pig iron plant and the pipe and creosote plants. And below them Kuhni's, where they cooked down dead animals for byproducts, the cement floors beyond the wide-open doors pooled and smeared with rich blood, men with long blood-slick aprons at work with long knives. The biggest dog in the world stood chained and guarding the way, in the back a twenty-foot-high pile of animal bones, where magpies and black winter crows fed.

The close, surrounding mountains gave everything a feeling of permanence, even isolation, as if nothing could enter or leave Utah Valley. The Utah valleys were Zion, a place of protection and safety. Out of Utah and beyond the mountains, as we boys had been told so often in church, lay the harlot Babylon, with all her enticements, which we, at the risk of our eternal salvation, must avoid, although there seemed little chance of being enticed at the time. Though we might hike ten miles in a day or bike twenty or even thirty, we weren't likely to go too far astray. Of course, there was always the possibility of thumbing a ride or hopping a slow freight to faraway places.

With one father in three out of work, WPA crews digging water-line and sewer trenches in the streets, and federal relief checks and commodity handouts and church welfare the only salvation, ambition seemed somewhat unrewarding, even excessive. Our greatest desire was to turn sixteen, be licensed, and then at eighteen graduate from high school, never have to go to school any more in our whole lives, and join the army and go to war.

A high school graduate might expect to go to college, if his family had money, but few families did. Because of so little money, few Mormon missionaries were going out to proclaim the gospel to the waiting world, find the blood of Israel, and be led to the honest in heart, so that wasn't too much of an ambition either. We boys didn't talk about going on missions much.

We were on our own and expected to entertain ourselves, our play and our lives copies of our older brothers and older neighborhood boys, their information of what to do and when given to us without our even knowing it was happening. Play was not organized, except for the Provo High School varsity basketball and football teams.

No one seemed ambitious for us. We were not often urged to compete, to rise in the world, because there wasn't much for a boy to rise to, except perhaps to the status of an Eagle Scout. It was hoped that someday we might get a job and be able to pay bills. Being able to pay your bills was very important. On the radio at nights, listening with our parents, we heard the Hindenburg go down, heard *War of the Worlds*, and heard President Roosevelt reassuring the whole Depression-defeated nation that they had nothing to fear but fear itself, later seeing these events in *Life* magazine's black-and-white pictures and in Movietone News films. Adequately fed, clothed, housed, largely free, seekers of our own pleasures, we boys were not afraid. The approaching world war only intrigued us, filled us with the hope of eventually being old enough to join the military and fight.

Hiking in the east mountains, far above Provo on summer days, five or six of us together, we sat on high ledges, drank from canteens, and looked down at our familiar town, if there was a breeze. Otherwise, the smoke from the coal stoves, Ironton, the pipe plant, and railroad yards obscured the view, sometimes covering the valley in a layer of smoke. But on clear days we saw the small towns, each a cluster of dark trees connected by Highway 89, and the band of dark trees along the river, the shimmering polluted lake, the west mountains beyond, the patchwork fields, railroad yards, BYU, downtown, the high brick smokestack from the burned and destroyed Woolen Mills, and the thirty or so square blocks of the Sixth Ward, the yellow-brick ward house visible among the trees.

And yet in our heart of hearts we wished that the pioneers had never come, that the valley lay as it had for centuries, populated only by Indians, smoke drifting up from their villages, their teepees pale in the afternoon sunlight. We wanted to see herds of buffalo, antelope, elk, and deer, see mountain lions, and the solitary and dangerous grizzly bear, and packs of wolves. We wanted to be hunters and warriors, wear loincloths, carry bows, quivers filled with arrows, and lances with long obsidian points, or at least be mountain men and trappers dressed in buckskin and wearing coonskin hats and carrying our muzzle-loading rifles across our saddle horns and ever wary of Indian attack, or, barring that, be cowboys wearing two holstered ivory-handled pistols and riding splendid white horses.

Yet, sitting on our ledge looking down, pleased but not knowing why, we were glad that we lived there in this place and in this time. For, whatever adults may have thought, the Sixth Ward, Provo, and Utah Valley belonged to us boys, all of it accessible to us because we were largely free to roam as we pleased, as long as the police, sheriff, and truant officer didn't haul us in and we didn't maim or kill ourselves or each other, or otherwise interfere with adults and their dreary lives.

ward, baptism, deacon, salvation, sin

DEDICATED IN 1900, the brick Sixth Ward chapel, also called a ward house, meetinghouse, or house of the Lord, was on Third South between Second and Third West. Two and a half stories high and built of faded yellowish brick, the ward house had wide front steps leading up to the big double front doors and into a large assembly room filled with fold-up seats, also called the chapel. Here on Sunday all the priesthood holders, all males over twelve, met for an early meeting. Later was Sunday School, and in the evening sacrament meeting. Primary, the children's organization, met on Tuesday afternoon, and the Mutual Improvement Association (Mutual or MIA), the youth organization, met that evening. The Relief Society, the women's organization, met on Wednesday afternoon.

The top floor of the ward house was classrooms; the half-basement held the kitchen, more classrooms, the Scout room, the restrooms, and the recreation hall or cultural hall with a stage for plays and programs. Because my mother became the janitor and we had to clean up the ward house every week, I got to know it well, too well. After she divorced my father, to earn money my mother started taking in washings and ironings and going out as a cleaning woman, and she did the ward house too.

The women she worked for picked her up and brought

her home or gave her money for the Yellow Cab. She expected a cup of tea at ten o'clock, a nice lunch, and a cup of tea again at three. She worked for the wives of doctors, dentists, lawyers, and professors, but she never thought they were any better than she was. At supper she often told my two brothers, Rowland and Bob, and my sister, Marlene, and me stories about the families she worked for. They seemed like very ordinary people. I grew up thinking I was as good as anybody else.

The ward membership was a thousand, more or less, with seats in the chapel for a third that number of brothers and sisters, the clamorous pushdown seats in rows with an aisle down the middle. In front was the stand where the bishop, an unpaid layman leader of the ward, sat along with his counselors and the speakers, if it was sacrament meeting. If it was the opening exercises of Sunday School, the Sunday School presidency sat there. Behind the bishopric were the choir seats, piano, and push-pedal organ.

Above the choir were three ten-foot-high paintings done by Sam Jeppersen, a self-taught Sixth Ward painter. The right-hand painting showed a group of seated apostles and, teaching some seated Indians, the standing Prophet Joseph Smith, founder of the Mormon church and translator of the Book of Mormon from gold plates delivered to him by an angel. In the center painting the Prophet knelt in the Sacred Grove with God the Father and Jesus standing above him answering his prayer to know which church was true and telling him none of them. In the left painting Jesus sat on the steps of the temple in Jerusalem blessing the little children.

The Joseph Smith in the grove, who was supposed to be fourteen, didn't look like any fourteen-year-old kid I knew anything about. He wore a suit and was too old, but I didn't let that shake my faith necessarily. Heavenly

Father and Jesus looked okay. I didn't doubt that they appeared, but I wondered how they managed to stay up in the air. I didn't know much about gravity at the time, but it seemed somewhat improbable. Yet it wasn't a serious theological question for me that young. I used to sit in meetings and look up at the painting and wonder, though.

They baptized you at eight, so you were officially a member and capable of sin, although no one mentioned or celebrated the baptism event particularly. You got baptized in the font in the basement of the Utah Stake Administration Building on the corner of First North and First West, although you could be baptized in the river, the lake, or a canal, if that's what your dad wanted to do and there wasn't any other place handy. The font room was dark and cold, and the water was cold too. I got baptized on Sunday, and when I came out of the building I asked my mother if I could have a dime for the show, which she gave to me. That was my first official sin, I guess, because you weren't supposed to go to the show on Sunday.

I didn't go to any of my friends' baptisms, and none of them came to mine. In fact, I don't know if any of my friends ever got baptized. Maybe they didn't. They didn't always act like they had been. Maybe I was the only one, although this seems doubtful. We didn't talk about baptism as being connected with our eventual salvation. In fact, in spite of all our Primary and Sunday School lessons and the hopes and prayers of the sisters who taught us and told us to be good, persuading us with cookies and other treats, we didn't talk about salvation at all. We were too young and interested in our own lives and small pleasures to be interested in salvation, ours or anybody else's.

Boys were known to sneak into ward houses that had

their own baptismal fonts, fill the font, and swim naked. The Sixth Ward not having a font, my friends and I were never guilty of such sacrilege.

Before you were baptized at eight, you weren't accountable for your prior sins, however terrible they may have been, but all future sins had to be repented of. We boys had a vague idea of sin, or at least of certain sins, the Boy Scout Oath and Law adding to this list when we became twelve and Tenderfeet. Lying, cheating, swearing, and stealing were official, certified boy sins. We knew we weren't supposed to swear or cuss, but we took a rather liberal view of that sin, allowing ourselves certain indispensable terms. Other words like *birdbrain, moron, jerk, chicken, dimwit, boob, sissy, ninny, crybaby,* and *freak,* words we used in communicating with each other, didn't come under any known prohibition. We also had our own somewhat liberalized interpretations of what it meant to lie, cheat, or steal. The word *steal* was pretty much absent from our vocabularies; we preferred *thug, swipe,* or *lift.*

You were supposed to kneel by your bed every night and morning to say your prayers, but it was too cold in the winter and too embarrassing generally, although I said short standing-up prayers for things I needed desperately, like a dime to go to the show or help to catch a limit of trout or hit a home run playing softball. And you were always supposed to be building your testimony so you would know the gospel was true.

Violations of the Word of Wisdom, a law of health by way of commandment, were particularly serious sins for a boy—drinking tea, coffee, or alcoholic beverages, or smoking, or eating too much meat. We boys got lots of priesthood and Sunday School lessons on the Word of Wisdom. If you saw somebody smoking, going into a saloon, coming out of the state liquor store with a bottle wrapped in a brown bag twisted tight around the neck, or drinking a cup of coffee or tea in a restaurant, you knew with absolute certainty that person was a sinner. I never considered my mother's tea drinking as sinful, for, as she explained, she was English and needed her tea to keep her going.

But we boys saw no real need to repent unless we were caught committing sin, an arrangement that seemed reasonable. We were sometimes told we were supposed to be clean and pure. But when we were younger, no Sunday School or priesthood teacher or Scoutmaster ever defined that particular requirement in any graphic detail, and we were reluctant to ask. We were often told that we were wet behind the ears, something else adults said that didn't make any sense.

Grandma Thatcher knew about sin. A heavy, imposing woman whose word was law, she often used the word *wicked*. Various things were wicked for my grandmother. Hearing a story about some misdeed, she would say, "Wicked, wicked," shaking her head. To be called a wicked, wicked boy was a terrible experience. She would also show her disapproval by clicking her tongue and shaking her head. Merchants, doctors, dentists, and repairmen who charged too much were called daylight robbers. A girl who went wrong was a baggage, or little baggage, and a boy in the same category might be called a wastrel.

English and stubborn, she and my grandpa would sometimes not talk to each other for three or four months and occasionally a year, but they would talk through the ten children. Yet they slept in the same bed and eventually reconciled their differences. Grandpa would bring home a small bag of candy, which he called a little sweetening for the bird, and put it on the kitchen counter. If Grandma didn't throw it out the door, he knew the coast was clear.

The Sunday after you were baptized, in sacrament meeting you went up on the stand, were told to sit in a chair, and then the bishop, and your dad, if you had one who held the Melchizedek Priesthood, which my dad didn't because he wasn't a member, and some other lay priesthood holders laid their hands on your head. Your head heavy and warm under eight or ten hands, you listened to yourself being confirmed a member of the church, being told to receive the Holy Ghost, to follow his guidance. You were urged to be faithful and true and keep all the commandments, go on a mission, get married in the temple, multiply and replenish the earth, and inherit the glory and kingdoms prepared for the righteous who had endured to the end.

In the blessing you might even be reminded that you first existed as an intelligence and then as a special spirit child of God prepared to come to earth in these latter days to receive an earthly body prepared by your parents to help build the Kingdom. You were told that you were eternal, had lived forever, and your whole family, clear back to Adam and Eve, were concerned about you, and knew what kind of boy you were, and watched over you. And they would be waiting at the veil to receive you when you passed from this life into the glories to come, so you had to keep on improving and perfecting yourself and become a god too eventually, if you wanted to.

I knew that mothers had babies, although I didn't know the particulars involved and nobody seemed inclined to tell me, which was okay with me at the time. But I didn't exactly know what receiving the Holy Ghost meant or how it felt or if I could hear or see him even if I tried. I knew he was supposed to be my constant companion and teach, protect, guide, and inspire me and generally smooth the way, which seemed okay, because I was beginning to think I wanted to be a good boy, within limits, although I was careful not to mention this to my friends. I would need all the help I could get.

I knew that the Holy Ghost was a still, small voice, but I didn't know how I could hear him if he was still, which I assumed meant silent, but maybe it was possible. I decided that small meant little, but it seemed strange that somebody as important as the Holy Ghost would have a little voice, because he might even have to holler sometimes to make me and my friends hear. I believed by this time that in the next life I would remember all my sins and that everybody else, all my dead family, friends, and neighbors, especially my mom, would know them too, which did help somewhat to keep me in check. But then I would know all their sins too, which would help make it not quite so embarrassing.

I also believed there was a special heavenly angel whose special assignment was to keep a written record of everything I did, writing the good things, if I did any, on one side of the book and the bad on the other. At night going to sleep, I sometimes thought about what this angel might have recorded that day, which tended to keep my behavior reasonable. Dead relatives could serve as guardian angels to watch over and protect you. My mother often appealed to my guardian angel in my behalf. I guess she thought I had only one.

I knew that Jesus liked fishermen and that he knew where the best fishing was and told fisherman where to throw their nets, which made me like him. I became very concerned about catching a lot of fish, which I knew took faith and even prayer, just like gaining strength to overcome your sins. And I knew that when you were older, the patriarch would lay his hands on your head and give you a patriarchal blessing just for you alone, which would tell you which tribe of Israel you belonged to and all about what your life would be like if you were righteous and kept all the commandments.

In Primary after you were nine, boys were in classes without girls. We were Trekkers, Trail Builders, and Blazers. We had to earn cloth badges to glue on our neck sashes called bandalos, and, hair combed, standing in a row, we sang, "Oh, we are the Boy Trail Builders out west where the sunset glows, where the brooks flow down like silver from the heights of the virgin snows," except we didn't know what *virgin* meant and never thought it important enough to ask. Probably it meant white.

If you had a birthday during the week, you brought your birthday pennies, a penny for every year you were old, to put in the Primary Children's Hospital bank, which was shaped like a small hospital. You dropped the pennies down the chimney. While you stood in front with the other kids who had birthdays, the whole Primary sang "Happy Birthday" to you. Even boys looked forward to bringing their birthday pennies to Primary. But our mothers didn't celebrate much. I was never invited to a friend's party. Birthdays didn't seem very important. You might get twenty-five cents by your plate at supper, a cake with candles, or a small gift, but that was about it.

Boys had a lot of ward meetings to go to, if we were faithful or our mothers made us go. It was very important to be faithful. Before we were twelve, we had to go to Primary on Tuesday afternoon, and after we were twelve we went to Mutual and Scouts on Wednesday evening. On Sunday we had Sunday School in the morning just like everybody else and the dreary two-hour-long sacrament meeting at six in the evening. And once we were twelve and received the Aaronic Priesthood, which they always called the lesser priesthood for some reason, and were ordained deacons by the laying on of hands, we had to go to priesthood meeting, which was before Sunday School. It took a lot of faith. As a deacon you passed the sacrament and on Fast Sunday, the first Sunday of the month, collected fast offerings, when all the brothers and sisters fasted two meals and gave the saved money to feed and clothe the poor.

Our teachers all through Junior Sunday School and Sunday School were nearly always sisters—Sisters Grimett, Oldroyd, Gray, Weight, Harris, Hafen, Jones, Nelson, and Thompson. Boys didn't have brethren teaching them until they got into Scouts and Aaronic Priesthood at twelve. In our church lives, at least until we were twelve and even after, the sisters were more important than the brethren. They seemed to work harder to keep us on the straight and narrow and were more personal and warmer than the brethren. Even the brethren themselves, bearers of the Melchizedek Priesthood, said that the Relief Society sisters were better organized than they were and were the people who really ran the Sixth Ward.

We knew that outside the valleys and across the mountains was a place called Babylon, or the sinful world, from which the pioneers had fled to build Zion in the tops of the mountains, and which we boys were to avoid at all costs, although we weren't sure why, except it was sinful and the Babylonians would try to lure us into sin.

After Pearl Harbor and so many men being drafted and enlisting, we boys knew that if servicemen came home on furlough drinking and smoking, it was a sure sign they'd been out consorting with the Babylonians and lured into sin. The side of Webster's grocery store had a big painted sign of a camel and a package of Camel Cigarettes, and the sign said, I'D WALK A MILE FOR A CAMEL." In my younger days, I thought it meant they'd give you a real camel if you'd walk a mile, which I thought very generous, although I didn't know what I'd do with an animal like that if I had one.

4

hot water, screen door, backyards, flies

ALTHOUGH MY MOTHER, two brothers, sister, and I lived in three other houses in the Sixth Ward, our house on Third West between Second and Third South was the house where we lived the longest, from my third through seventh grades. I don't know where my mother got the money to buy the house, because we were broke. Maybe my Uncle Harry Heal, a successful real estate man, helped her get some kind of deal.

Every month I had to take the house payment of twenty-two dollars down to an old lady who lived next to my Grandpa and Grandma Thatcher and have her sign the payment book. My mother warned me that if the payment was a day late, the lady could repossess the house. The old lady was thin and old and struck me as mean. I didn't like her. She never gave me a cookie or a piece of candy for bringing the payment. I thought she should have.

The Sixth Ward was an old part of town. Most of the houses were brick, or sometimes stucco, or occasionally frame, but frame wasn't trusted. Wooden houses burned, rotted, had to be painted, and took more work to keep up. Some of the houses were two stories and had once held large, faithful pioneer families. But these families were gone, the houses divided into apartments, some of the bigger houses empty, the windows broken, the rooms filled with trash.

At night we boys, slightly frightened, entered these haunted houses to move from room to room hoping to be terrified by monsters, ghosts, murderers, or escaped State Hospital maniacs. The windows in these derelict houses were meant to be broken with rocks. Every neighborhood had at least one haunted house.

Our house, a yellow stucco, had two bedrooms, a front room, a bathroom, a kitchen, and a glassed-in summer porch, all heated by coal stoves, which was fairly typical for a Third West home, except my mother rented out half the house and we lived in the other half, sharing the bathroom with the renters. Marlene and my mother slept in the bedroom, and Rowland and Bob and I slept on the summer porch.

All the houses on Third West were old, not pioneer houses but old, maybe forty or fifty years. Pioneer houses always had lilac bushes and hollyhocks growing in front. My friend Dave Nelson lived in a pioneer house made of adobe brick. I envied Dean Gray, who lived next door and had a furnace, a room of his own, overstuffed furniture, carpeted floors, and a piano.

Some Sixth Ward backyards were trashy, overgrown with weeds, but some had vegetable gardens. Richard Tucker's dad always kept a beautiful, weedless garden, watered from a small artesian well so he didn't have to use irrigation water, which always brought weed seeds. Some houses had artesian wells, the water with a wonderful iron taste. Along the road going down to Utah Lake were two big, flowing artesian wells into which you could stick your whole face and head to cool off and get a drink.

Few yards had back lawns. Some neighbors had chickens in their coops, but most were empty, smelling faintly of long-vanished chickens and dust when we boys entered. Chickens were kept for both eggs and meat. Playing in the backyards, you sometimes saw one or two headless chickens, their feet tied to the clothesline so their blood would drain out. My dad used to buy live chickens and kill them. He soaked them in a bucket of scalding water to loosen the feathers, the hot, wet feathery smell quite unpleasant.

Old sheds, garages, cowsheds, and small barns stood unpainted and neglected in the deep backyards. We boys knew and investigated all these structures in our search for hideouts, treasure, and the satisfaction of being where we weren't supposed to be.

A house might have central heating, but most of my friends' houses didn't. Many houses had a coal stove in the kitchen, used for cooking, warmth, and heating hot water in the tank attached by a pipe. A potbellied stove in the living room, if you had one, was strictly for heat. Little kids had to be taught not to get too close to the potbellied stove, its sides sometimes glowing red. If you saw kids with big burn scars on their faces, arms, or hands, you knew how it happened.

Some of a boy's main tasks in life were to keep the coal scuttle full and be sure there was kindling to start the fire in the morning, and to put coal on the fire when asked or to poke the fire to get it going. And of course the ashes had to be carried out and dumped on the ash heap and not in the trash, because that was a good way to start a fire with hot coals and maybe burn the house down eventually.

In winter you were constantly warned to shut the outside doors quickly and not let out the heat, because coal cost money and your parents weren't made of money and money didn't grow on trees. Similar warnings applied to turning out the lights. We knew that our parents weren't made of money. Obviously they were flesh and bone. And we knew that money didn't grow on trees. At least if it did, we hadn't seen such trees, although we kept our eyes peeled.

Because of the daily need for hot water, fire for cooking, and heat in winter, the kitchen stove was kept burning all day. Your mom often told you she'd been slaving over a hot stove all day when she was trying to get you to do something, and you ought to be appreciative. The only way to cool the house was to keep the windows and doors open, all of which were screened to keep out the flies. There were lots of flies. You often heard, "Don't stand there holding the screen door open and let in all those flies."

Boys were notorious for letting in flies. To kill flies, you used Flit, a sweet-smelling fly killer in a sprayer with a pump handle, the pink Flit in a refillable glass bottle screwed into the bottom, and you used fly swatters and long curls of sticky tape hanging from the ceiling. It was a great pleasure to spray Flit for flies. You kept pumping until the whole room was full of a faint sweet-smelling pink mist, a film on the kitchen table and counter, wet-winged flies dropping in mid flight, yourself a little woozy. It took a lot of Flit.

The long curl of tape covered with stuck dead black flies was a visual daily warning of a kind, but you were never sure of what, probably something to do with sin. Sin, as we boys well knew, was a very sticky proposition and was best avoided, depending of course on how much fun was involved.

You were also warned daily, hourly in the summer, not to let the screen door slam and otherwise not to cause a hullabaloo. Your mother was always saying, "Now what's this hullabaloo all about?" But we didn't know, although we liked the sound of the word and liked to say it over and over again—hullabaloo, hullabaloo, hullabaloo. Powered by a long coiled spring, a screen door could slam with a sharp bang, upsetting your mother, waking baby brother or sister or your sleeping father, who was on graveyard out at Ironton or the State Hospital. We boys were famous for running out to play or go to school and letting the screen door slam shut. In the winter the concern was to keep the outside door shut and not let the heat out, a relatively serious crime. In this regard a boy was often asked if he was raised in a barn or if he was trying to heat the whole outdoors, which we obviously weren't. We were just going somewhere lickety-split and forgot.

During the long winter nights, the kitchen and front room stoves went out and had to be rekindled, something usually your dad did, if you were lucky, or your mom. You didn't usually keep the potbellied front room stove lit during the winter day, so the only heat was in the kitchen when you woke up to go to school. Bedrooms and bathrooms were always cold, the windows coated with thick frost, the lit kitchen stove the center of life. It was a great comfort to dash out of your icy bedroom carrying your clothes and dress by the kitchen stove, your toes curled against the still-cold linoleum floor. You didn't stray far from the kitchen stove's warmth. It was important to be warm.

5

tomato soup, brutality, dancing, nosebleeds, fire escape

THE FRANKLIN ELEMENTARY SCHOOL was on Third South and Seventh West. Three stories high, the Franklin, a square, brown-brick building with creaky wooden floors and stairs, sat in the center of its own block, along with a new white two-story addition. The school's most significant feature for us boys was a covered winding fire escape slide from the top floor on the east side of the old building. There was no ladder, so to slide down you had to climb up, which was slippery and hard to do and was best done in bare feet, but you had to be careful somebody didn't run off with your shoes and socks. Sliding down was wonderful, except if some boy had peed down the slide, which some boys liked to do, although I never did, as far as I can recall, although I certainly understood the temptation.

The Franklin covered kindergarten to sixth grade, and then you went on to the Dixon Junior High School for three more years, and then to Provo High School for another three. Because our older brothers and sisters, even our parents and aunts and uncles, had attended these schools, we knew the teachers' names and who was to be feared because of work or discipline and whose class you didn't want to get into. But there was little choice. Mothers didn't arrange to get you into the class you wanted.

You went to school and took your chances. You could get held back at the end of the year, which was terrible because then you were a year behind all your friends and everybody knew how dumb you were. You had a homeroom teacher in whose class you spent most of your time, except in the sixth grade when you marched out for instruction in music and dance.

There was no particular brutality at the Franklin, but it was obvious to the boys, although perhaps not to the girls, that their parents backed the teachers. A boy might expect, if he acted up or became unruly, to have a teacher grab him by the shirt collar or ear to take him out of class and have him sit in the hall. Or he might be seized by both shoulders to have some sense shaken into him, or slapped, or cracked on top of the head with a hardwood yardstick most teachers kept readily at hand. We were often warned that we would have some sense shaken into us. I didn't know exactly how that worked, but I suppose it worked in certain instances.

If you got slapped or rapped with a yardstick or otherwise punished, you didn't mention it at home, for there was little sympathy. It was assumed that you got what you deserved, that as a boy you were born to misbehave, and you might learn to behave the next time, maybe, or somebody might give you something else to cry about. We should just as well grin and bear it. "Stop being such a baby and try to be a man" was an admonishment we boys often received.

If you were sent, or taken, to the office, it was to see the principal, not a counselor. There was no counselor. Boys didn't need to be counseled, they needed to learn to behave or be in fear of getting their necks wrung. Getting your neck wrung was a common threat. Chickens got their necks wrung. Or a teacher might send a note home with you, which could lead to dire consequences.

The note had to be answered, so you didn't dare not deliver it.

We boys feared the Franklin men teachers more than the women, who were often reasonably kind if not unduly provoked. But there was one young, beautiful music teacher a boy might expect to be kind but who was, in fact, rather mean and strict. One day a boy, a Christensen kid, sitting in one of the front desks in my music class did something that annoyed the beautiful teacher. She grabbed him by the hair, lifted him half out of his seat, slapped him across one side of the face with the palm of her hand and then, with great efficiency, across the other side with the back of her hand. Released, slowly his head sank forward onto his desk and he began to cry, but not loudly, as the beautiful teacher went on with the singing lesson.

The most feared teacher at Franklin was the principal, Mr. Emol K. Nielsen, who also taught the sixth grade. Awkwardly tall, thin, always dressed in a black suit, he was quick as a cat and swift to administer justice. For a boy to be in Mr. Nielsen's class was considered a form of doom. We had all heard from other older brothers, and even our sisters, countless stories of Mr. Nielsen's swift and sure attack.

You were, of course, instantly identified as related to your older brother, if you had one—and you usually did, several probably. As one of those Thayer, Rhodes, Oldroyd, or Nelsen kids, you were reminded publicly on the first day of class that the teacher had your number because he assumed the boys in a family were all the same. So if your brother had been a troublemaker, and he probably had been, then you didn't have a chance, which was another cruel fact of life we had to deal with.

The kindest teacher was the fifth-grade teacher, Mrs. Edmunds. She rewarded the class with a peanut bust if we

all got a hundred on the spelling test. Twice I was responsible for the class not enjoying the large bag of peanuts. I
wasn't attacked on the playgrounds for my deficiency, but
I was warned severely on both occasions, which resulted
in improved scholarship. It was a great pleasure to sit at
your desk and crack, one by one, a neat pile of peanuts
with your teeth, tasting the woody husk and then eating
the meaty kernels while listening to Mrs. Edmunds read
a story, which was also part of the reward.

If there wasn't snow or rain, recess was for jacks,
hopscotch, jump the rope, tag, pop the whip, and marbles, although boys didn't ordinarily play jacks, jump
the rope, or hopscotch, all girls' games to be avoided unless one wanted his essential maleness to be questioned.
Marbles was a boy's game; girls didn't play marbles,
although they might be allowed to watch. Some boys
became great players, carrying their winnings around
in a bulging sugar sack. Competition was fierce. Every
player had his favorite taw, or shooter.

Players lagged to see who went first. It wasn't unusual for an expert player to clear the whole ring of marbles,
not giving his opponent a chance. We boys all knew who
the best players were. I was not a good player, repeatedly losing the small sacks of marbles I bought at Woolworth's at considerable expense. It was perhaps my first
hint that I would not be good at competitive athletics.

Fist fights were fairly common, all the kids forming
a circle to cheer and encourage mayhem, but the fights
were seldom dangerous and never fatal. A teacher always came along to break it up, take the two assailants
by the collar, and drag them into the principal's office.
I never saw or participated in a gang fight involving at
least half the boys in the school, but I'd heard that such
wonderful experiences were possible and were events to
look forward to.

You were ranked as a fighter, every boy knowing who he could beat up and who could beat him up. The list of boys I could beat up was not long. Thus I became polite, deferential, and self-effacing early as a means of survival. Adults, particularly women, assumed that my behavior, plus my being a Boy Scout, meant I was a good boy, even a nice boy, a side benefit I readily accepted as my due.

In winter, if we had a good snowstorm, we had mass snowball fights, half the school on one side and half on the other, girls included. As long as you didn't mold a rock into your snowball, which might put out an eye, this was not considered a dangerous activity. Your whole side organized, you made five or six snowballs and, holding them against your body with one arm, yelling and screaming you charged the other side, driving them from the field. We were brought in from recess by the office student running around the building ringing a big brass bell.

All the kids brought a lunch, unless you lived close enough to dash home. You ate at your homeroom desk, or, if you didn't bring a lunch and your folks were on welfare, like half of Franklin probably, you went down to a basement room to have a bowl of soup, usually to-mato, sitting at a table covered with green oilcloth. The smell of the oilcloth and the soup mixed so it tasted like you were eating oilcloth in your soup, or at least eating off the oilcloth and not from a bowl. The room was cold and a little steamy from the big pot of soup, but the soup was hot.

The school nurse came for half a day, but she was for nosebleeds, vomiting, bad headaches, fainting, schoolyard injuries, and to determine the early signs of measles, mumps, chicken pox, scarlet fever, and various other communicable maladies before the contagion swept through the whole school. She wasn't there to hold your hand. Kids often came to school sick, or almost sick. To be sent down to see the nurse wasn't unusual, unless you had to be carried.

Having virtually every disease known to man, including rheumatic fever, I was described as a sickly child but was reminded by my mother that most of my pains were growing pains and that I would eventually, if I lived, grow out of them. Boys didn't like going to the doctor for a physical examination and particularly didn't like being checked for a hernia, whatever that was, which seemed to us a gross violation of our dignity and a subject for considerable debate.

Dave Nelson had the most spectacular nosebleeds. He received no hint when he was about to start bleeding. The blood squirted suddenly from his nose all over his desk, Dave leaning slightly forward, the whole class watching, some pointing, the teacher rushing to help. It was as if he might bleed to death, turn white, and slump forward, although he never did. I envied Dave his nosebleeds.

A boy named Tub Larsen beat up on me occasionally, and Mrs. Edmunds made him sit in a chair and told me to hit him, which I really didn't want to do. Mrs. Edmunds told me to hit him harder, but I knew what would happen later if I did. Tub just smiled. He was fat. My feeble blows didn't hurt him. Two other boys were named Slug and Grub. Slug hit other boys. You had to watch out for Slug.

In the sixth grade we learned to dance. Most of the boys sort of liked learning how to do the foxtrot, waltz, two-step, Virginia reel, and other approved dances. We were also taught dance courtesy. To ask a girl in the class for a dance, a boy had to walk up to the seated girl and, with one arm across his stomach and one across his back, bow at the waist and say, "May I have this dance?" There was no holding the girl close. There had to be enough space to drive a pickup through. We boys danced somewhat flat-footed, almost dragging our feet. But we were game, most of us anyway.

There was no sense of anything sexual. Yet, it was the first time a boy received adult approval to hold a girl; that is, to put the extended right arm around her waist and hold her left hand in his and look into her face. Feeling the girl's dress, having the sense of the body inside the dress, was a curious, not-unpleasant experience, suggestive of some grander moments to come and that we were beginning to grow up, would at some far-off miraculous moment take on the role of lover and husband and the inevitable fatherhood. It was important to grow up, to be grown. Our parents and other adults often said they'd be glad when we grew up and got a little sense finally. We seemed to be remarkably without sense.

A boy really found out how many girls liked him only when he opened his Valentine box. Every kid had a decorated Valentine shoebox for other kids to put Valentines in. The boy who got the most Valentines was the most popular, which neither I nor any of my friends ever was. You had to say how many Valentines you got. You always checked the names on the Valentines to find out which girls liked you. It seemed important to be liked and by particular girls, keeping the name in mind for future possible reference.

At Christmastime choirs from visiting schools stood at the base of the stairs to sing carols. Teachers opened the classroom doors so we could all hear. Quiet, attentive, we listened to the songs like an echo coming up the stairwell. On May Day we wound the Maypole, a rather dubious activity for boys, holding onto a long colored ribbon and weaving in and out with smiling, laughing girls, who seemed already to know things about the purposes of life we boys were as yet unaware of.

6

hooligans, mumblety-peg, rock fights, breaking glass

AT TWELVE OR THIRTEEN, a boy, once he had his chores
done, was free on summer days to go pretty much anywhere in Utah Valley he could walk or ride his bike to.
It was expected that he wouldn't wound or kill himself
or get himself picked up by the police or sheriff because
of some felonious conduct and that he would be home
in time for supper. However, at ages nine, ten, and elev-
en, he and three or four of his friends—possibly more,
depending on what they were doing—stuck fairly
close to the thirty-block Sixth Ward neighborhood and
its environs, usually making it home for lunch and to
report in.

Included in this rich area were the Denver and Rio
Grande Western Depot and railroad yards, the hobo
jungle, millrace, tabernacle, Hotel Roberts, Provo High
School, Sixth Ward chapel, Clayton's and Webster's grocery stores, various backyards and vacant lots with their
barns and outbuildings, a haunted house or two, Pioneer Park, uptown (the ward's north boundary), Bandley's Car Repair, three lumber yards, a blacksmith shop,
Crane Maternity Home, two dairies, Troy Laundry,
Highway 89, Startup Candy Company, Provo Greenhouse, Utahna Gardens dance hall, and Provo Hide
and Fur, each with its attendant promise of activity and

purpose. It was a unique area, one filled with rich possibilities for enterprising boys whose rightful desire in life was pleasure.

Sixth Ward yards, running to the middle of the block or abutting another, with lawn or not, were all fenced in and, depending on the owner's seriousness, at different heights with various combinations of barbed, sheep, and chicken wire and boards. We boys knew which fences were climbable and where, vital information when trying to escape a neighbor's wrath or elude an enemy's pursuit. As each yard was named after the owner, a boy referred to the Oldroyds' yard, or the Madsens', Claytons', Tuckers', Menloves', or Grays'. Yard boundaries were strictly kept, not unlike the way the Mormon faith required observable limits.

We knew who would shout at us and order us away: "You kids get out of here! I'm calling your mothers! I know who you are, and don't think I don't!" Or the more dire threat: "I'm calling the police right now! I've warned you before. I'm not putting up with this hooliganism any longer!"

An irate neighborhood sister in the gospel always called us by our family names—you were a Thayer boy, or Rhodes, or Nelsen, or Hodson—and not our first names, which she didn't know unless she'd taught us in Primary or Sunday School. And these sisters were always going to tell our mothers of our invasion, never our fathers, as if our fathers had nothing to do with our behavior and general upbringing.

Our penchant for taking shortcuts or making a beeline somewhere aroused anger. Going to school, church, a friend's house, uptown, or otherwise exploring the possibilities of devilment, we always took shortcuts or made beelines. These, like hidden jungle trails, were essential to our desire to move fast, stealthily, and unseen.

Somebody was always saying, "Let's take the shortcut" or "I know a shortcut" or "The shortcut's faster."

We were often called little devils, hellers, born hellers—which was worse than a plain heller somehow— or hooligans. *Hooligan* had a nice sound. I didn't mind being called a hooligan, although I didn't appreciate it much when an adult called us "little bastards"; somehow it seemed worse to be a little one rather than an ordinary one. I did have some sense of dignity. Even at that tender age, I'd looked up the definition in the dictionary, and I knew that my mom and dad had been married when I was born. I also assumed that my friends were legitimate, for I had no particular reason to believe they weren't, even if some irate male adult—irate women never seemed to use the word, for some reason—called that legal marital bond into question on what seemed to them appropriate occasions.

For some boy to suggest that your mother was a female dog was bad. Adults typically didn't use this term to describe boys, just other boys did that, and it meant you had to fight. It didn't matter how big he was or how old, you had to fight him or lose all sense of worth in the community. If he was bigger, it was permissible to use a rock, stick, piece of two-by-four, or anything else handy, but you had to fight, even if you got cold-cocked or flattened in the process, which meant you were rendered unconscious.

Yet, in Primary and Sunday School we were learning that our bodies were temples for our spirits. We didn't know exactly how that worked, but we knew it had something to do with the still small voice we were always supposed to be listening to and were much in need of being able to hear and follow if we were to be clean and pure and get to the celestial kingdom, the highest degree of glory, the one for which every brother and sister in the Sixth Ward was pining. There were three degrees, but only the celestial really counted and was the most desirable. If you were in the celestial, you could go down and visit your friends and family members in the telestial and terrestrial, but they couldn't come up to visit you and couldn't progress eternally and become gods who got to populate and run their own worlds.

On fast Sunday, the first Sunday of the month, when you were supposed to fast for two meals and give the money saved as a fast offering to help the poor, the Sixth Ward brothers and sisters got up to bear their testimonies about how they knew the church was true. They told stories about the sick healed, the dead raised, about long illnesses, straying family members brought back into the fold, missionary experiences, human folly, dreams, visions, pregnancies, new grandchildren, valiant pioneer ancestors, vacation trips to California and Yellowstone Park, and how they longed for the Second Coming, when the earth would be cleansed of all iniquity and they would inherit their mansions above in the highest degree of glory.

After church, cutting though backyards to get home and change clothes as quickly as possible, we boys saw the old sheds, corrals, chicken coops, and small barns with deer antlers nailed above the double doors. Weatherbeaten, unpainted, often derelict, they were leftovers from an earlier pioneer agricultural era. Although the cattle and horses were gone, some families still kept chickens, rabbits, and maybe one lonely cow.

A boy might steal an egg or two to sell at Clayton's store for a penny to buy candy, but he would typically not steal a chicken or a rabbit. That seemed too grave a felony. Having seen many cowboy films, a boy wouldn't think of stealing a cow. They used to hang you for that. He did, though, feel free to throw rocks through windows if the structure was obviously not being used. There was contentment in the sound of breaking glass.

Vacant lots belonged to us boys. We dug undergrounds with connecting tunnels, built forts, constructed cardboard towns, lit fires to roast potatoes, played games, and fought our wars on vacant lots. Nobody cared. Nobody even knew who owned them. They weren't worth that much. Undergrounds were at least six feet deep and covered with old boards and cardboard with dirt on top so they were secret. For light we got old oil from the service stations and made lamps with rag wicks. Using picks and shovels, we sometimes took a whole week to dig an underground.

Trees were very important to us, but the trees in the backyards were not high, not heavy-limbed and good for climbing, yet we made the best of what we had. We wanted a marvelous tree house like Tarzan of the Apes, with rope bridges between the trees and long vines to swing on above the lurking lions, pythons, crocodiles, and leopards. Walking through the thick trees along the Provo River, we kept our eyes peeled for hanging vines as a means of transportation and escape, so, like Tarzan, we'd be able to swing from one vine to another, yelling his Tarzan yell to tell Jane he was on his way to rescue her once again and to just hang on.

We liked to be off the ground, hidden, to have secret places in the trees that no adult knew about and where we could spy on people down below and across in other yards. If a kid you didn't want in the tree tried to climb up, peeing on him was always a sure defense, the malefactor screaming in agony as he jumped or fell back to earth, damp and odorous.

Before we were old enough to swim in the river or at the North Park Pool, we dammed the Third West gutter for refuge from the baking sun. We slid on the mossy cement bottom, had water fights, and raced cucumber boats. We even drank gutter water. It didn't seem harmful.

Strung to telephone poles, power and telephone lines crisscrossed the backyards, so that at night against the clear sky it looked like a spider's web of lines. Family clotheslines were strung from poles set for that purpose, sometimes two or three lines strung from one pole.

On Mondays, wash day for most families, the backyards were festooned with colorful clothes hanging from the lines—diapers, pillowcases, sheets, underwear, dresses, tablecloths, coveralls, overalls, Levi's, and socks drying in the hot summer sun, the clothes an index of the family's number, sex, prosperity, and general cleanliness.

In the evening, if there was a breeze and the white long-legged, long-armed suits of men's underwear were dry, they ballooned with air, ghosts dancing against the darkening sky. Mormon sacred underwear called garments hung from the lines; you had to go to the temple in Salt Lake first before you could wear garments.

In your roving through the Sixth Ward neighborhood and beyond, you ran with boys your own age, perhaps a year younger or older but no more than that. Bigger boys threw rocks at you if you tried to follow them, or they threatened you with mayhem. Particularly your older brother didn't want you trying to run with his friends, younger brothers being, as they were, a burden and an embarrassment. Having your ears cut off was a fairly common threat, the older boys taking out their pocket knives and opening the longest blades, although I never saw an earless neighborhood boy.

Before they started school, boys often wore coveralls, in grade school they wore overalls, and in junior high Levi's or jeans, so everybody knew how old you were just by looking at you. The worse thing when you were five or six was to wear knee-length brown stockings held up by garters. A great indignity.

On a summer morning you didn't phone your friend before you went to his house because, like you, he probably didn't have a phone, nor did you ring the doorbell or knock on the door; you stood on his front porch and hollered his name until he or someone in the house heard you. You were either invited in or told to wait until your friend came out. Always dubious about younger brothers' friends, older sisters typically told you wait. Why this was so I never understood. When your friend finally appeared, behind him his mother's voice called after him, "Now you behave yourself today."

"Sure, Mom."

"Just see that you do."

"Sure, Mom."

Once he was safe out the door, the inevitable question was, "What do you wanna do?"

Still in the sixth or seventh grade, we were too young for summer jobs, even picking fruit, except maybe strawberries or raspberries, so, free of school, the whole day lay before us. We had no plans particularly from one day to the next, didn't part the previous evening with the next day all laid out. We'd sit on the front porch maybe to talk and then decide who else we wanted to go with us to do whatever we were going to do. Or we didn't decide but rather drifted into some activity, keeping our eyes peeled for anything that promised a reasonable degree of pleasure or diversion. We were pretty much on our own. We did not play basketball or baseball; they were boring.

If later in the day your mother wanted you for any important reason, she stood at the front or back door and shouted your name until you answered, or she might

send a younger brother or sister to discover your where-
abouts with a message to come right home, making life
that day difficult.

We might start out the day searing ants with a magni-
fying glass or burning holes in newspapers. Or we might
just throw ice picks and pocket knives at trees, or take
off our shoes and socks and stand in a circle barefooted
and play a version of mumblety-peg. An ice pick was
easier to stick up than a pocket knife. I never actually
saw a boy's foot pinned to the grass, although it was a
hoped-for possibility. Ice picks didn't make big holes. If
you jumped out of the circle first, you were chicken. We
spent a lot of time calling each other chicken.

Lined with shade trees and gutters on both sides,
Third West, also called Depot Street, ran from Fifth North
all the way down to the train depot on Sixth South. Third
South, which was half a block down from our house,
was also Highway 89. All the truck traffic and travelers
to or from Colorado, Arizona, Nevada, California, and
beyond came up or down Third South.

Sometimes we boys sat under a shady tree out of the
glaring sun to watch cars pass, naming and identifying
the cars and the out-of-state license plates. The boy who
yelled the name first won. It was an interesting and edu-
cational thing to do and resulted in many arguments and
accusations of being blind as a bat or blind in one eye
and not able to see out of the other.

At our play, we boys listened, without knowing, for
the great boom of an accident on Third South. Sponta-
neously dropping what we were doing, wanting to be
there before the cops, we ran instinctively toward the
sound, anxious to see smashed and overturned cars, broken glass, leaking radiators, and the strewn and bleeding bodies, if we were fortunate, the wail of approaching
sirens adding to our pleasure.

Accidents were high drama, particularly if a fire hydrant had been knocked over so there was a geyser to add variety. The gathered adults shook their heads, the mothers standing with their arms folded across their chests and always shooing us back so we would not see the injured and dying, the pooling blood. Later the closest neighbor washed this away with buckets of water from the hose or ditch and swept up the broken glass with the kitchen broom. After everyone was gone, we boys returned to the scene to see the stains, pick up the small, broken metal pieces of cars, and talk about life and death.

Or we might on any given morning walk the block over to the millrace. Coming out of the Provo River, the millrace flowed through the brickyard, down Second West, under Center Street to Second South, where it emerged again and continued down under the railroad yards, through the CCC Camp and the golf course to finally join with the Provo sewer.

Trout and minnows came down from the river. We fished for the trout through a manhole on Second West. Sitting around the manhole, we dropped our baited hooks into the water, sometimes three or four lines down at one time, and waited under the summer sun. Some kids were very successful fishermen, Bob Liddiard and Elaine Christiansen in particular. But I never caught one trout through the manhole, perhaps an early indication of the disappointed and passionate fisherman I would eventually become, a prayerful boy of weak faith.

A street lamp stood where the millrace emerged from the culvert, and at night, crawling up on hands and knees, we looked down to see the shadowy trout that had emerged. We built gigs out of broom handles and forks but never succeeded in harpooning any of these trout.

Barefooted, overalls or Levi's rolled up, we seined the millrace's mossy stretches for minnows and bullheads, which we put in a Spry can filled with water to take home and leave on the back porch. In the morning the minnows were all belly-up and inevitably dead. In the fall when the water was cut out of the millrace, we searched through all the pools and under the culverts under the roads for stranded trout.

In the spring the millrace was a small torrent, full from bank to bank, swift and deep. One afternoon my friend Jim Rhodes and I got a heavy piece of broken cement to throw off a wooden bridge on the count of three. But I let go too soon, and Jim, better at arithmetic, was still hanging on and went into the water with the cement and could easily have met his doom. He survived, but, wary of Mrs. Rhodes's wrath, which Jim duly reported to me, I didn't dare go by his house for a week or two.

Mrs. Rhodes believed that I'd tried to drown her darling boy, which was not my intention at all. I liked Jim, and besides Mrs. Rhodes made wonderful chili and tamales, and Jim's Aunt Minn worked at Startup Candy Company wrapping chocolates, and sometimes, if we were in that neighborhood, we would inevitably suggest to Jim that we go visit Aunty Minn, a friendly and generous woman, at her task. When my Uncle Harold was a boy, he worked at Startup trapping mice and rats, a penny for a mouse and a dime for a rat.

I thought this would be a wonderful job, to move through the darkened storage rooms checking your trap line, taking out the dead animals, dropping them in your sack to be counted later and paid for, your wealth growing, then resetting the traps. Uncle Harold had a dog Shep, his constant companion, who caught rats, which helped make Uncle Harold rich. Uncle Harold was much to be envied.

7

big buck contest, sparrows, shot and killed, saloons

ALTHOUGH WE WERE TOO YOUNG to hunt deer, in September boys watched the close east mountains for the first leaves to start turning and the first skiff of snow on Mount Timpanogos, the highest mountain around, which meant fall was coming and the duck, pheasant, and deer seasons. There was no age limit for fishing, but you had to be fourteen to hunt birds and two years older to get your buck license. We knew the exact spot below Maple Flat where every year the first maple leaves started turning orange and red, and we watched that spot. Higher up among the pines and spruce, the quaking aspen started turning yellow and it was colder in the mornings and the air smelled sharp and clean.

As the opening of deer season got closer, construction workers, truck drivers, service-station attendants, and other men who worked outside a lot started wearing their red hunting hats and sweatshirts, the sweatshirts sometimes torn and blood-stained. Some men wore their hunting knives to work, but they didn't carry their rifles. Sears and other stores ran whole-page ads in the *Herald*, with pictures of ducks, pheasants, and trophy buck heads at the top, advertising guns, ammunition, and other hunting equipment, except during the war when ammunition and new rifles and shotguns were hard to get.

Carlson Sporting Goods advertised their big buck contest, and articles appeared describing that year's hunting prospects. In September, sometimes in late August, someone always set the dry Mud Lake bull rushes on fire, or maybe it was lightning or spontaneous combustion. If we were hiking in the east mountains, we saw the leaping line of flames, the plume of white smoke, and we knew that the hunting seasons were coming.

We hunted sparrows in neighborhood trees, carried our .22s and shotguns with us into the hills on our hikes, but the real hunting seasons didn't start until the fall. We all knew that. We hunted jackrabbits all year round. There was no season on them; they were pests, something to be exterminated. When we were sixteen and somebody had a car, we drove out west of the lake to form long lines and jump the rabbits and kill them with shotguns and .22s, blasting away, shooting all our shells, because there were lots of jackrabbits.

T-shirts off because of the summer heat, six or eight boys in the line going through the waist-high sage, we tried to push the rabbits up against a hill so we could see to shoot them. A .22 was best because we could see the slugs kicking up the dust so we could adjust our aim, the big thrill when the running jack folded and rolled. You yelled and hollered because it was so great.

Nobody ate jackrabbits; we just ripped off their tails to keep count. At night we drove the dirt roads with a boy on each fender to shoot the jacks as they ran across in front of us or stood paralyzed by the lights. Some nights we killed fifty or sixty rabbits using this method. Cordon Cullimore had an old Ford convertible that was great for night hunting, but you had to be a little extra careful not to shoot anybody riding in front. Some boys went at night with their dads to the city dump to spotlight and shoot rats, but none of us was so fortunate.

Walking down through the fields during the summer, we always watched for pheasants and flights of ducks. We'd heard of poachers who soaked corn in whiskey and scattered it for the pheasants. The poachers waited until the pheasants got drunk and fell down, and then just went out and picked them up and put them in a gunnysack. We wanted to try that just to see how a drunken pheasant acted, but we had no ready access to whiskey.

A lot of fathers hunted deer during the Depression. It was important to bring a deer home to bottle or to cut up into steaks, chops, and roasts to put in your locker at the ice plant. Some men got special doe permits so they could shoot two deer, or they bought permits for their wives and shot their deer. Unless you shot a doe for the meat, you didn't shoot does. You could shoot a doe on your regular permit if you wanted to, but it was too easy. Only cowards shot does. You didn't tell anybody if you shot a doe. You didn't want to be a doe killer.

A real hunter shot a buck. They were smarter and harder to get, and their antlers made them dangerous if a wounded or cornered buck turned on you, but ordinarily they didn't do that. Sometimes if the buck wasn't dead and the hunter bent over to cut its throat and it jumped up, it might knock him down. There were stories of hunters straddling a deer to cut its throat, and when it jumped up the hunter rode it down the mountain hanging onto the antlers, his companions somewhat surprised when he galloped past them in full flight.

We liked the deer season because you could sell the deer hides down at Provo Hide and Fur, a good hide bringing up to fifty cents if the buck hadn't been dragged and most of the hair worn off. We kept our eyes peeled for hides that obviously nobody wanted, draped across fences or tacked to the sides of garages and barns.

Every year hunters got shot and killed. Sometimes

a hunter thought he was shooting at a deer, or maybe his gun went off accidentally. But sometimes a hunter would just be standing on a ridge, and a bullet meant for a deer a mile away killed him instead. It was strange to think of a bullet in the air coming right at you.

At the beginning of the season, signs appeared outside neighborhood markets quoting prices for cutting up deer, although a lot of hunters cut up and wrapped their own deer. Saturday afternoons if you were near the foothills, you heard the sounds of rifle fire as deer hunters sighted in their rifles, which you could do just above town. You didn't have to go to a shooting range. We kept watching the mountains and hoping for an early frost so the leaves would fall off the oak and maple brush and the quaking aspen. You could see the deer better when the leaves were off.

At school we talked about where our dads hunted deer and if they'd got a big buck last year and where they were going this year and if we got to go with them. It was important to shoot a big buck with wide, high antlers. You measured the spread in inches, and you counted the points only on one side. Real hunters shot only four-point bucks, and really good hunters shot five-point and six-point bucks. It was all right to shoot a three-point if that was the best you could do, but if you shot a two-point or a spike you weren't proud.

If your friend's dad shot a big buck with bigger antlers than your dad, it meant he was a better hunter and perhaps even braver. Fathers nailed antlers over their garage doors or sometimes on an old telephone pole in the backyard, where they kept antlers from all the bucks they'd ever killed, the old antlers bleached white in the sun. For each set of antlers there was a story.

In service stations, lumberyards, machine shops, and saloons, antlers and mounted heads hung on the walls.

And you always asked who shot the big buck and where, and you heard the story. Snapshots of hunters kneeling by big bucks hung on the walls by the cash registers or were taped under the glass on the countertops, so you looked down at them. And there were snapshots of men standing behind rows or piles of pheasants, ducks, and geese. Saloons always had mounted deer heads above the mirrors behind the counters.

Standing in the saloon doorways, we saw the men at the bar drinking beer and looking up at the heads. There were also big calendars and beer advertisements with pictures of beautiful women carrying guns or maybe standing by a big buck they'd killed. The women didn't look like they were dressed for the cold fall weather, but they were always smiling and looked like they were happy. Sometimes in the background you could see a tent with hunters sitting around the fire drinking beer and smiling or sometimes just holding up the bottles of beer to look at them, the beer was so good.

Sometimes fathers didn't take their sons with them on the deer hunt but went with their comrades, men they'd hunted with for years, always returning to the same favorite place, the men laughing and talking as they loaded their pickups, already describing the great hunt they were going to have. They were sometimes gone for a week, sometimes even hunted on Sunday, which faithful, exemplary priesthood holders weren't supposed to do, their disappointed sons waving to them from the front steps as they drove out smiling and happy. The wives, sometimes pregnant, or perhaps holding a new baby, or maybe just standing there with their arms folded across their chests, shaking their heads, turned and walked back into the house.

8

perfection, mumps, castor oil, clinics

As my friends and I grew older, we began, as boys will,
to be aware of ourselves as persons. You began to have
a sense of having a body, of wearing clothes, of having
and wanting possessions, of seeing and remembering
things, of being capable of sin and transgression, and of
people noticing you and saying you were growing like a
weed. They never said like a tree or even a bush or maybe a flower, but always like a weed, which you didn't
like to think of yourself as, because you'd pulled a lot of
weeds in your dad's vegetable garden, so you knew how
highly weeds were regarded. But sometimes they said
you were a fine boy or a nice boy, although it was mostly
the Sixth Ward sisters who said this and not the brethren,
for some reason.

About this time I personally saw the benefit, as a
member of the one and only true church in the whole
world, of being good, or at least trying. Adult brothers
and sisters in the gospel liked you better, again particularly the sisters, if they thought you were good, meaning
that at least some of the church teachings were actually
taking effect, finally. They complimented you and held
you up as an example, and so you could get away with
more sometimes.

I don't remember any of my friends saying they

wanted to be good, and I certainly didn't mention my decision. One sister told me that she knew I would never swear and that should I ever be provoked or feel inclined to, I should simply say, "Oh, sugar!" Given my companions, it was advice I feared to follow.

My mother told me that I had been a good baby and would sit tied in my highchair staring at the wall for two or three hours at a time and not making a sound, something I may have seen as an early tendency in the direction of goodness. Later, at twelve and thirteen, a Boy Scout and a newly ordained deacon in the Aaronic Priesthood, I would aspire to perfection, a condition an inexperienced, prepubescent youth should perhaps leave to the aging, who have more cause and motivation to improve what remains of their sinful lives.

Although healthy and active for the most part, we boys sometimes found ourselves diseased or wounded, or both. Measles, mumps, chicken pox, scarlet fever, whooping cough, rheumatic fever, polio, flu, sore throats, tonsillitis, infected ears, appendicitis, broken arms and legs, sprains, cuts, blood poisoning, and lockjaw — there were various possibilities. The city health department put a big sign on your house for communicable diseases, so everybody would know you were quarantined.

If you had something mild like the measles or chicken pox, some neighbor mother might bring her four or five kids over to your house to expose them and get it all over with at the same time, because they were going to come down with it anyway. You were always coming down with something. You didn't get sick, you came down with something, as if coming down were different than getting or being sick.

You didn't go to the hospital unless you were at death's door; you went to the Clark or Hasler Clinic. Doctors Nixon, Clark, Hasler, or Merrill or some other family doctor made house calls to check up on you. Pretty much every boy had his tonsils out and maybe his appendix, both operations happening at a clinic, not the hospital. We boys expected to have our tonsils out. It had something to do with rendering you nontoxic.

If you had your appendix out, you had to stay in bed for ten days with your whole body taped from your groin to your chest, and you couldn't have any water for the first three days. The nurse just soaked your lips with wet cotton or gave you ice chips to suck on.

Because my mother was broke, as she often was during those lean Depression days, after Doctor Stan Clark Sr. took out my appendix, I spent my ten bedfast days in the Utah County Infirmary. A dark three-story brick building located in the foothills between Provo and Springville, it was in fact the county old folks home. I lay in a room with three ancient men, who I assumed were sick and dying, for they never spoke but only on occasion groaned. The church paid for my surgery, but who paid for my hospitalization remained a mystery. It was probably free. The church also paid for three operations on my mother's feet, or she wouldn't have been able to walk, which helped convince me that the church was true.

Those first three days after the surgery, I grew so thirsty that I seriously thought of drinking from a vase of flowers resting on the bedside table and would have, had I not thought it would bring a more painful death than I was already suffering or that the flowers might die. When Dr. Stan Clark Sr. stripped off the four-inch-wide adhesive tape in quick fast jerks, I screamed bloody murder, which is what you screamed if you were serious. Just screaming wasn't enough.

But appendix removal aside, we didn't complain much unless we dropped in our tracks and couldn't go out to play. To ward off various maladies, we got a daily tablespoonful of cod liver oil from a bottle shaped like a fish. You might get an aspirin or a slug of cough medicine that had a sweet, hot taste and wasn't bad at all, but it was rationed because it contained alcohol and could lead to early drunkenness and addiction. A dish of vanilla ice cream or a chocolate malt from Cook's Ice Cream might be used to keep you aware of the pleasures of this life and away from death's door.

A dose of salts or castor oil was a common dreaded remedy, but an enema was worse than slow death. Mothers believed in purging their sons when necessary. If you looked a little peaked, your mom put her hand on your forehead to test for fever and then reached for the thermometer to see if it was serious. For sore throats and chest colds, you got a Vicks VapoRub, an alcohol rag pinned around your throat, or a mustard plaster, a treatment that left something like a third-degree burn on your chest.

Your mother painted minor cuts and scratches with iodine or Mercurochrome; more serious wounds were treated with sulfa drugs. We were constantly warned about the dire consequences of blood poisoning. We feared lockjaw perhaps worst of all, for we had heard tales of the afflicted having their front teeth knocked out with a hammer so they could be fed through a tube. We sometimes practiced locking our jaws and talking through our teeth just to get the feeling of what it would be like.

We also feared polio; we had no desire to be locked in an iron lung for the rest of our lives with only our heads sticking out. We wondered how you could go to the bathroom if you were locked in like that. More than any approaching pain or even death, we feared the indignity of having to use a bedpan or urinal. Being ruptured was also bad, although it was still somewhat of a mystery how that happened. We often described each other as being ruptured.

Boils were bad too. We often had boils. Carbuncles had to be lanced by the doctor, but your mother popped ordinary boils, pierced them with a needle sterilized with a lighted match, or used the vacuum of a heated bottle to draw them to a head so they could be popped or pierced, all the time telling you to hold still and not be such a boob, or the reverse of that, to be a man, depending on the mood she was in. We were told that a boil was the meanness coming out, which we assumed might be true, so we didn't argue. Girls didn't seem to have boils.

Our somewhat frequent broken arms required a plaster-of-Paris cast running from elbow to wrist and weighing perhaps five or ten pounds. More serious fractures required casts running the full length of the arm and from the chest to the belt, or perhaps from the belt to both ankles, weighing perhaps twenty or thirty pounds. A heavily casted boy who was still ambulatory was admonished to avoid getting close to deep water.

If you were sick, you usually lay on a couch or daybed in the kitchen, where your mother could keep an eye on you and nurse you through the illness. If it was summer, the shouts and yells of your friends came through the open screened windows and door from the backyard, where you longed to be. Our mothers were our nurses, with the help of other neighborhood mothers who were called in because of some special knowledge or experience.

For difficult cases the family doctor came to the house. And the elders, Melchizedek Priesthood holders, might also be called in, and perhaps the Sixth Ward bishop himself, to anoint your head with the sacred oil and lay their hands on your head. And they blessed you that your body would be healed and the angel of death would pass over you, so you would grow to be a righteous, faithful young man with a strong testimony of the truthfulness of the church and serve a mission. And after that become a husband and father, multiply and replenish the earth, and fill the measure of your creation, and serve faithfully in the church your whole life long.

Our mothers didn't tolerate our malingering or complaining to any great degree. Much of our suffering was attributed to growing pains. The typical admonishment was, "You'll grow out of it." And you would, of course, if you didn't perish first. Continuously in pain from her own crippled feet, my mother's favorite comment on my pain was, "You'll sure die of it," which I assumed I might, being a boy prone to the tragic view of life.

Headaches and other insufferable boyhood pains were treated with an aspirin, or paregoric if the pain was sufficient, or perhaps an ice pack, or a hot-water bottle. For stomach ache you got a cup of medicinal tea, really quite delicious with sugar and milk but not counted as breaking the Word of Wisdom, or you got something to clean you out. We did not like to be cleaned out. If the pain was severe and unending, your mother would relent of the purgation and take you to the doctor. A ruptured appendix was something to be feared.

The only immunization was vaccination for smallpox, which raised a mean, painful sore on the upper arm if it took, producing a heavy scab and a lifelong scar the size of a nickel. You didn't punch a boy in the arm for weeks after he'd been vaccinated. Of course, swimming in polluted Utah Lake was a form of immunization, although we didn't recognize it as such. If you could survive the lake, you could survive most diseases known to man.

Old people were cared for at home mostly, although they might go to the county infirmary or even the State

9

fudgesicle, Royal Crown, Cook's, Startup's trash

ON SUMMER DAYS we boys needed gum, candy, soda pop, ice cream, and donuts to sustain life. So if it was early enough in the morning and we thought we could get there first, we'd ride our bikes up to the A&W drive-in to pick up trash left on the parking lot from the night before. For this, two or three boys each got a frosted mug of root beer, a most delicious and soothing drink, but you had to be there early.

Or, we might go up and search in the clothing-store trash bins for shirt boxes to take to Dalebout Bakery for a sack of day-old donuts. Dalebout's had an exhaust fan that blew the bakery smell out onto Center Street, just to torture boys. The trash at Startup Candy Company was always a possibility for nourishment, for they sometimes threw out stale candy bars, the chocolate turned white but perfectly edible. Fruit of Paradise was my favorite, but Opera Bars and Cherry Sundaes were good too.

Bob's Billiards on University Avenue and Hank Smith's on the corner of First West and Center were our favorite pool halls or saloons, although we were forbidden entry and knew they were dens of iniquity. Yet it was pleasant to stand in the open doorways, breathe in deep the smell of beer and cigarette and cigar smoke, and hear the click of billiard balls and the low murmur

of contented men standing at the bar drinking yellow beer and conversing about important things.

A boy with a pool-hall father was allowed to enter if his mother had sent him on payday to retrieve his dad or get money for the weekly groceries before it was all spent. The best approach was to walk up to your father and pull at his shirt or coat sleeve until he put down his beer or pool cue and turned to look at you.

My father's favorite pool hall was Hank's, the biggest in town, with splendid twenty-foot-high ceilings layered with bluish cigarette and cigar smoke, and around the walls on shelves stood dusty mounted mule-deer bucks looking down through glass eyes.

After my mom and dad were divorced when I was six, my dad lived just a half a block away from Hank's in the back room of an old hotel called the Royden House. His responsibility after the divorce was to pay for our haircuts and shoes and sometimes to provide our show money. Every fall he cooked for Hank Smith's deer camp and got all the deer hides for me and Rowland and Bob to sell, which we loaded onto our wagon and took down to Provo Hide and Fur. He also filled a tub of water and helped us wash our whiskey bottles that we'd gathered to sell to the paint stores for turpentine containers at twenty-five cents a box. If we caught a bunch of catfish, he'd drive a nail through their heads into a board, cut around their necks, and skin them.

You might hit up your father for a nickel or a dime, because you knew he probably felt guilty being in a pool hall anyway and he wouldn't want his beer-drinking, pool-playing cronies to think he was tight, so he'd probably give you the desired coin and tell you to get the hell out of there and what were you doing the hell in there anyway, because it was no place for you. Which was okay because you understood perfectly.

Foraging along Center Street, we three or four boys might check out all the sidewalk grates to see if somebody had accidentally dropped a nickel or a dime or maybe even two bits, a coin that had rolled into the grate and was unretrievable without special equipment.

What you needed was a long stick, a piece of chewed gum, and a match. You rolled the gum into a ball, stuck it on the end of the stick, and then lit the match—a boy always had a few matches in his pocket for emergencies—and heated the gum to make it sticky enough to pick up a coin.

It wasn't often that we found money in the grates, but it was always worth checking at least once a week. You had to have faith. I knew that two bits was a quarter, four bits fifty cents, and six bits seventy-five cents, but I never understood why you didn't say eight bits for a dollar.

We collected beer and pop bottles for the penny refund, but as a salable commodity all boys knew about, they weren't easy to find. Provo Hide and Fur bought all the brass, copper, and aluminum we gathered, so we were always on the lookout for these precious metals. Any aluminum pot resting on a back porch was considered thrown out and our rightful possession. Too young yet to have summer jobs, we had to exploit every source of possible income.

We held a very low opinion of the Elks Club, because they smashed all their empty whiskey bottles, which we considered a great loss to us personally. They weren't fooling anybody. We spent a lot of time digging through uptown trash bins. We knew which side was up. To accumulate that weekly pile of glass, Elks had to drink like fish, my mom's favorite expression when describing drinkers. We boys worried more about our loss of revenue than about the Elks breaking the Word of Wisdom and not making it to the celestial kingdom, which they didn't seem too interested in anyway.

With a nickel three boys could buy and share a candy bar, usually a Baby Ruth or Butterfinger, or a milknickel, popsicle, or fudgesicle, each boy getting a bite until the confection was gone. But you had to take the same-sized bites, and you were carefully watched.

"Come on, you took too big a bite. You cheated. I get two bites."

"You're crazy. I didn't either."

"Oh, yes you did."

We got into fights sometimes, but not often. Because every boy knew who could beat him up and who he could beat up, there wasn't much point in fighting really, unless the offense was particularly grave. If you were sure of yourself, you might say, "I can beat you up any time I want."

"Oh, yeah?"

"Yeah."

"I'll knock your teeth down your throat."

"Just try it."

If things did come to blows, there were rules. No biting, kicking, kneeing your opponent in the groin, hitting below the belt, no use of sticks or clubs, no sharp instruments, no putting out eyes. You didn't really want to knock out any teeth either or have yours knocked out, because then your mother would know you'd been in a fight, and you didn't desire that. Flowing blood, usually a bloodied nose, was a signal to stop because blood had been shed, and that was a sign of bravery and could be repaired before you got home, unless you got blood on your shirt. A black eye was also a badge of honor.

It was all right to bawl as long as you kept slugging, because you didn't want to be called a sissy or a boob, which was bad. If you had a big brother, you could invoke him and say he'd beat up on your opponent, unless, of course, he had a big brother too. Usually after the fight, you were friends again at least by the next day and ready for new activities.

If, with our communal nickel or dime, we went down to Cook's on Center Street between Fourth and Fifth West, easily the best ice-cream store in Provo, and bought an ice cream cone, we took turns taking licks. If you happened to see a friend walking along eating a fudgesicle or some other delicacy, you hollered, "Bites!" which, according to our laws, entitled you to a bite. He might tell you to get lost, but, on the other hand, he might prove ethical.

A bottle of pop was another possible communal purchase, each boy taking his swallow or slug in turn. We sometimes bought a Coke, a Pepsi, or a Nehi Orange, but usually a Royal Crown Cola because the bottle was bigger. A package of gum, easily divided into sticks and half-sticks, presented less occasion for controversy.

If we couldn't come up with a nickel, maybe only three or four cents, we bought penny candy. A jawbreaker or an all-day sucker was the best buy, although a Tootsie Roll, bubble gum, or a big gumball was acceptable. One didn't usually have to share penny candy. An egg was good for a penny's worth of candy; the source of the egg was never questioned. Even if your folks didn't have chickens, several of the neighbors did. We called this activity lifting, thugging, or sneaking, not stealing. We didn't like to think of ourselves as thieves. We had aspirations of becoming Boy Scouts in a year or two and knew all about being trustworthy and morally straight.

If you wanted to gamble, you could go to Kirkwood's, a little drugstore on Fourth West, where punchboards were available. The temptation of winning a whole box of chocolates was almost irresistible, but to not win and lose your nickel was a terrible experience, so the punchboard was to be approached with considerable caution and resolve.

The ultimate gastronomical experience was for five of us to get together a dollar and go up to Joe's Spic and Span on First West and First North and purchase a sack of ten hamburgers, but the cost made this a very rare event. The Spic and Span was always filled with the wonderful smell of frying hamburgers and onions, old grease, coffee, and cigarette smoke. Another good place for hamburgers was Snappy Service on University Avenue.

These money-earning or money-acquiring ventures were important. They not only provided us with treats necessary to our well-being but also built trust, cooperation, and an entrepreneurial spirit.

10

telescope rod, Sears, planters, browns, luck, limit

BOYS IN THE SIXTH WARD who fished were divided into two categories, those whose fathers fished and took them along and those who were on their own, like me. This had far-reaching consequences in terms of instruction, equipment, and fishing trips. However, both groups of boys fished together on weekdays. Special fishing trips with fathers happened primarily on Saturdays, or, if the father was not a faithful Latter-day Saint, on weekend trips, unless the father fished primarily with his cronies, as some fathers did. The men that a husband fished or hunted with were typically referred to as cronies, not friends, by his wife. The fortunate sons also got to go fishing in Yellowstone Park and other exotic places.

Our need to fish was instinctive, primordial, passionate, a driving force that had to be satisfied, something not to be questioned or explained, something surging in the blood, as was hunting. Of course, not all Sixth Ward boys fished. They found themselves possessed by other passions.

The first fish we caught were minnows seined in the millrace and the ditch on Fifth West where it flowed through Pioneer Park. The first big fish were carp and mud cats in Utah Lake and the still water of the Provo River where it flowed into the lake. Limited as we were to the waters we could walk or ride our bikes to, our development as fishermen could be seen as a progress from the lake and the lower river up to the upper river, where it flowed, clear and sweet, out of Provo Canyon.

As a boy whose father didn't fish, I had no adult to introduce me to the required equipment and teach me the necessary techniques. Richard Tucker, across the street and two years older than I was, liked to fish, and at first I fished with him. Tucker's father fished, so I learned from Tucker and by trial and error, primarily the latter. As a boy I was never a competent trout fisherman, a fact that caused me considerable anguish and tested my religious faith.

My first experience catching big fish involved carp. My mother rented half our house to a young couple, and one day the husband and I walked the three miles to Utah Lake in the heavy summer heat to club carp. Moving slowly, very slowly so as not to cause ripples, you sneaked up on the carp in the shallow, smelly swamp water, their backs exposed, and hit them with a club. We brought home a string of three or four big carp. With their heavy yellow scales and pig mouths, they were not beautiful fish. It was the Depression. People were hungry, but carp were still trash fish.

The first truly edible fish we caught were mud cats and bluegills found in the still water the half-mile before the Provo River emptied into the lake. But even they were not totally satisfactory fish. We knew that real fishermen caught trout. Every summer Carlson Sporting Goods put a glass-lidded ice chest outside the front door on University Avenue, where Mr. Carlson displayed big trout, six-pound, seven-pound, and eight-pound rainbows, German browns, and natives, beautiful, magnificent fish caught in distant mountain reservoirs, lakes, and rivers. Standing in awe, filled with desire, we looked down at these trout, reading the tag saying where the trout was caught, by whom, the date, and the trout's length and weight.

When we went to service stations, garages, lumberyards, and barbershops, we saw snapshots of smiling men and boys holding strings of big trout or one man or boy holding up one huge trout. We saw Fisher and Coors calendars with beautiful women fishing; these fisherwomen wore nothing but their fishing baskets and hip boots and a smile, a big fish at the end of their line, of which they seemed oblivious.

Mr. Tucker, Mr. Liddiard, and other fishermen in the ward told us stories about fishing, especially how great the fishing used to be years before when they were boys or when their fathers and grandfathers were boys, the fishing getting worse with every passing generation. At the top of Provo Canyon, you came out into Heber Valley, and that used to be the best fishing, the Provo River flowing slowly down through the pastures and fields. Fishermen drifted dead minnows through the big, deep holes for giant browns, four-pound and five-pound browns being common. Browns were meat eaters and liked minnows. But the government was building Deer Creek Dam up where the meadows used to be, so the fishing was ruined. A lot of fishing seemed to be ruined and not like it used to be.

As beginners we learned that fishermen had secret fishing places that they never told anybody else about, and you couldn't ask because it was a secret. Secret creeks in secret canyons filled with fish, secret holes on the Provo River, and secret places in the reservoirs where there were lots of fish. And there were secret lures and baits and secret ways to fish, so we learned slowly that fishing had a lot to do with secrets.

The Rexall Drug Stores printed a calendar every year

that included a fish symbol to indicate which days would be good for fishing. We always checked the calendar. The best day was if the fish symbol was completely filled in. A fish symbol that was only half filled in wasn't a very good day. We believed in the calendar.

Most fishermen had one special hole they fished on opening day, the first Saturday in June at five in the morning. You had to be there early, maybe at two or three, to get the hole. But I didn't have any hole that was good enough to be special, so I just rode my bike up to the river below the mouth of the canyon, an area called Carterville, or maybe over to Spring Creek near Springville, or Brown's Creek, a canal that flowed out of the river.

Mr. Bee from Stephen Bee Hardware fished Brown's Creek. He had a long pole, and he would stand way back so as not to scare the fish, and he would drop his night crawler in the moss pockets. He caught more fish than any of us kids. Mr. Bee was very short and bald. He was a saddle maker. We used to stand and watch him at Bee's sewing on a saddle and breathe in the wonderful smell of leather and beeswax. We heard that one cold winter day he got caught in a big snowstorm while hunting ducks and dug a hole in a large manure pile and stayed there all night nice and warm.

All the fishing stories we heard were about big trout, never about lesser fish. We boys whose fathers didn't fish heard of wonderful, distant waters where these fish were caught—Fish Lake, Strawberry and Scofield Reservoirs, Provo River high in the canyon, and the Uinta lakes, waters teeming with big trout. In *Outdoor Life*, *Field and Stream*, and *Sports Afield*, the hunting and fishing magazines we read standing at the magazine rack at Bonnett-Vasher, our Center Street corner drugstore, we saw pictures and read stories about incredible fishing trips for trout in Wyoming, Colorado, Montana, and

Idaho, but not in Utah. A dry, hot desert state, Utah was
a good place to live if you were religious, but it didn't
seem like a good place to catch trout; however, we didn't
let this discourage us at the time. We had faith.

Strawberry Reservoir was the best place to fish in
Utah. Real fishermen had boats to troll for the big natives or cutthroats. Or they fished live minnows with big
cork bobbers, and when the big natives hit the minnow,
the bobber would go under and you knew you had a
big trout. Or the fishermen cast spoons from shore to the
passing schools of natives, their dorsal fins sticking out
of the water they were so big, the fishermen running to
keep ahead of the school. Strawberry was a wonderful
place, but it was fifty miles away up Provo Canyon.

Some fishermen had cabins and took their wives,
who canned the trout in pressure cookers on the wood-
fired stoves. However, most of the time men didn't take
their wives fishing with them, preferring their cronies of
long acquaintance. And if they weren't good members
of the church, they fished on Sunday, drank beer, played
poker, smoked cigars, and ate thick steaks at night in the
cabins, most of which activities were sinful and would
inhibit their joy in the next life unless they repented.

Going fishing early in the morning, I liked pedaling
my bike through the sleeping neighborhoods. I liked
pedaling out of town and through the fields, everything
cool in the early dawn, and hearing the robins and other
birds singing, and smelling the cottonwoods and the river. Being alone, I took more interest in things. It was the
first time I'd ever thought of things as being beautiful.

Sometimes in the hot afternoon, if I'd had another
discouraging day fishing, I took off my clothes and went
swimming in a deep river hole. If I couldn't catch fish, I
wanted to be down where they were, be like a fish maybe. There was some satisfaction in that.

For us boys, our equipment was typically a metal telescope rod, a cheap reel, cotton line, a leader, hooks, and
a basket. We didn't buy hip boots. We waded in an old
pair of shoes. Our Levi's dried out on the way home. The
telescope rod pulled out in three sections, but you had
to be careful because they bent easily and then wouldn't
telescope, so you carried the rod half pulled out and
slightly bent. We knew of split-bamboo rods, silk lines,
automatic reels, fly fishermen casting long distances to
rising trout, but we were bait fishermen; we fished with
heavy, fleshy night crawlers, a big worm that came out at
night and that you caught using a flashlight. Sometimes
we fished with spinners.

Weekly during the summer, we walked or rode our
bikes uptown to trail through Sears and the sporting
goods stores and look at all the rods, reels, lines, fishing
vests, and lures. The most expensive lines and reels were
kept in the enclosed-glass counter, where we could only
look at them. And we began to understand that the best
fishermen, the most expert, were fly fishermen.

We wanted bites in every hole, on every cast, letting
the night crawler drift down through the hole. Getting a
bite, waiting, waiting, until we were sure the trout had
taken the bait, and then striking, hooking the fish — this
became one of the most thrilling experiences of our lives.
And then feeling him on the end of the line, the feeling
coming up through the line to the rod and into the hand
and arm and whole body.

We never knew how big the hooked trout would be
or what kind, but we always hoped for a five-pound
brown at least. But this never happened. On a good day
fishing in Carterville, a boy might catch one or two ten-
to-twelve-inch browns or maybe a limit of ten-inch rainbows, if the State Fish and Game tank truck had planted
fish and he got to the hole first. If he was not able to catch

a limit of browns, his greatest hope in life was to hit a planted hole that nobody else had fished.

Planters bit fast and without caution, the same fish biting two or three times until you either caught him or nicked him with the hook so that he grew wary. Much smarter than rainbows, browns bit only once. Drifting a night crawler down through the hole filled with planters, you got bite after bite, finally satisfying your desire for bites and for catching fish.

But we knew that planters weren't a prize trout like a brown. They were raised in cement ponds at the Springville Fish Hatchery and fed ground-up meat from Kuhni's byproducts plant. When other fishermen asked if you'd had any luck and you showed them your small rainbows, they shook their heads.

"Looks like you got a couple of planters, kid."

There was no praise in their voices, no admiration. Their own baskets, black with dried blood, held two-pound and three-pound browns, their tails sticking out. Filled with envy, you turned away.

Luck. Fishermen always talked about luck. You had to have luck.

"Had any luck, kid?" Or, "Doesn't look like you've had much luck, kid."

I became preoccupied with luck. I knew you had to have luck. But I wasn't sure what luck was, only that I didn't have any, or very little. While fishing, I said silent standing-up-with-eyes-open prayers, promised exemplary behavior, promised to obey all the Scout laws if only I could catch a limit, catch a big brown, have luck.

Limit was an important word. You didn't count as a fisherman if you didn't catch a limit, which was eight trout. Men talked about limits, how quickly they'd caught a limit, or how often, and how big the trout were.

We caught limits of the small planters if we got to

a good hole first, but never of Carterville browns. We knew that the Fish and Game tanker had to stay on the roads, and we knew where the road came close to the river, so we fished those holes and the holes by bridges. We looked for tire tracks; we watched for the truck, chased after it on our bicycles to see where the trout would be dumped. And we listened eagerly for reports of fish tankers headed for the river, inquiring after all the relevant details.

Feeling a great need to see trout, to know that many trout existed, we walked, rode our bikes, or thumbed a ride the three miles to the Springville Fish Hatchery to see the trout and to fish Spring Creek, which fed the hatchery and then flowed under Highway 89 and down through the fields. Walking along the cement ponds, we looked down at the thousands of trout. Some ponds held big five-pound and six-pound spawners, incredible fish.

Some boys, overcome with desire, cut the bottom out of their right-hand Levi's pocket and, standing at the edge of a pond, dropped a baited hook to the ravenous rainbows below. Pulling the flopping trout up into their Levi's leg, they walked off stiff-legged. Although sorely tried, I never fell to this temptation, prayed for the strength to resist. Although I mostly prayed for things I wanted, I did on occasion plead for forgiveness or to avoid sin altogether, to the extent that might be possible.

At night I prayed lying in bed, eyes closed, thinking my prayer that I would catch a limit. I got up early to be on the river first, but I lacked faith. I moved too quickly from hole to hole, didn't fish each hole carefully and thoroughly, believed that the next hole would be filled with hungry, easily caught trout. I tried more sinkers, put on two night crawlers, but these remedies didn't help.

Summer evenings, sitting on my front porch or playing in the streets, I saw neighbors come home from fishing trips, usually to Strawberry or Scofield. Unloading their gear, they opened their coolers for us kids to see their trout, the cooler half full of big rainbows and natives, beautiful long, heavy, gleaming gold-and-silver fish. And their sons, my friends, described the trip and how great the fishing had been.

"We couldn't keep them off the hook—could we, Dad? We threw the little ones back. I caught the biggest, didn't I, Dad?"

I crept away. I had been invited to go to Scofield once. I'd never been fishing where you couldn't keep them off the hook. The place I wanted to go most was the Uinta Mountains, with more than five hundred alpine lakes filled with fish. According to the stories, you could catch a fish on every cast. You built log rafts to fish from, went out to the deep part of the lakes where the most fish were. And you had wonderful camping spots by springs and went swimming and saw deer in every meadow, and it was so beautiful you couldn't believe it. I believed it. I also longed to go to Yellowstone Park, where every fish was at least three or four pounds.

Fishing was my first experience with the turmoil of unrequited passion.

work, laziness, rotten laziness, damned rotten laziness

BEFORE WE WERE OLD ENOUGH to have summer and part-time jobs, we boys had chores. These included bringing in coal and kindling, emptying the ashes, filling and emptying the washer and wash tubs, setting the table, washing and drying dishes, cutting the front lawn, raking up the back yard, washing windows, emptying the pan under the ice box, making our beds, and watering the lawn, which you did by holding the hose or scooping buckets of water from the ditch. Boys didn't typically have a room of their own, so keeping it clean wasn't a problem. There were no assigned chores, no lists; you just helped when you were told to, unless you could get out of it some way.

My mother believed in three grades of laziness—lazy, rotten lazy, and damned rotten lazy. Her religion was work; work cured nearly every ill, stopped every complaint. She wasn't fiercely independent; we were on state welfare, and she accepted help when offered. But her gospel was work. If you were sick, you went to work if you could stand up and manage to get out the door. She was crippled, had what amounted to club feet, toes and feet covered with corns and calluses, and was in constant pain, but still she worked. Sick or well, she worked and expected us children to do the same, and without complaint. We were often reminded that work wouldn't kill us, which proved to be true, although at times we grew skeptical.

All the Thatchers worked. They might be guilty of various crimes and misdemeanors, but laziness wasn't one of them. Laziness was an absolute disgrace. There was no graver insult than to be called lazy. I never heard any of my uncles or aunts ever described as lazy. The Thatchers brought this work ethic with them from England. It was a lean family. In England, Grandpa Thatcher had a job in a foundry, but with ten kids to feed, there wasn't any great surplus. My uncles and aunts used to run to meet my grandfather coming home from work to see if he had left a piece of bread in his lunch bucket.

Grandma Thatcher counted the thin slices of bread each child got at supper, and there was no argument. She took in washing and ironing to help keep the family fed and clothed, with a roof over their heads, these being the three necessities. Three of my uncles were crippled, had a kind of shuffling step, although they could walk, and my mother always said it was because they were malnourished as children and suffered from rickets.

Although a lot of men were out of work during the Depression, most of my friends' dads seemed to have jobs, ordinary jobs. They worked out at Ironton, Pacific Pipe, or at the State Hospital, or for the railroad, or for the telephone or gas company, or in town somewhere, or for the city, state, or federal government, all eight-to-five jobs, and got paid once a week. Those who didn't have regular jobs worked on WPA projects digging sewer and water lines, whole gangs of men in the streets digging the long six-foot-deep trenches with their picks and shovels.

Pick-and-shovel work was considered the least skilled and hardest of manual labors, and you were warned that it was what you would end up doing for the rest of your natural life if you didn't get a good job, the rest of your natural life being somehow longer and worse than just your life. Working on the railroad as a section hand laying track was also considered quite limited. You were expected to rise above these two jobs. You were constantly told you needed to amount to something, but you were never told what; there didn't seem much to amount to.

I was ten when my mother took on the job of janitor of the Sixth Ward meeting house. She still went out to clean for other women, but she did the meeting house too. Her standards were high. No half-measures would do. She would send us back to do a particular task over a second and a third time if it wasn't done right. Robert and Marlene were too young to help much, but Rowland and I weren't. I felt unduly persecuted. None of my other friends had to work as hard as I did cleaning the ward house.

All the hundreds of folding seats in the chapel had to be dusted each week and all the sixty or so wooden chairs in the Relief Society Room too, every rung. And they all had to be moved back so the floor could be vacuumed properly, because the sisters quilted and they left a lot of thread on the floor. The vacuum cleaner didn't pick up well, and sometimes you had to get down on your hands and knees to pick up individual threads by hand. All the white wooden benches in the basement classrooms and the cultural hall had to be scrubbed with a scrubbing brush and Dutch Cleanser every several months.

The sacrament trays had to be polished and the cups washed. The sacrament was served in silver-plated bread and water trays, thirty-six small glass cups per tray. We usually washed them on Monday after school, each cup washed individually with the index finger in a cloth dipped in Dutch Cleanser to be sure they were clean. If left over a day or two, the water evaporated, leaving a ring.

The cultural hall in the basement, used for ward dinners, parties, and plays, measured seventy-five by a hundred feet with a wooden floor. My mother mopped and waxed this floor on her hands and knees. It took a whole day. Finally, I convinced her I could do it with a mop and bucket, but it took a lot of convincing. She thought I couldn't do it well enough. One of the reasons she liked to scrub floors was because she could rest her feet.

I didn't like cleaning the meetinghouse, but I began to learn what it meant to work, that a job had to be done right or it wasn't worth doing. Knowing that the ward house was all clean and ready for Sunday meetings and that I'd helped wasn't an entirely unsatisfactory feeling. I worked hard because my mother worked hard and because she was always in pain. I became very concerned about that pain. I thought if I worked hard I would somehow help stop that pain, at least some of it. I'd already begun to think I would become a foot surgeon so I could operate on my mother's feet.

I gained some satisfaction from my mother telling me I'd done a good job. Rowland and I didn't get paid. Part of my mother's pay was a grocery order at the bishop's storehouse, a church-run grocery store for needy members, on First North across from the post office. Pulling home my wagon filled with groceries so we wouldn't have to starve was something else that convinced me the church was true.

To be described as not having a lazy bone in your body was a great compliment. You were expected to work your fingers to the bone if necessary, give a good day's work for a good day's pay, and pay your own way. According to my mother, to be lazy was to go looking for work while all the time praying to God that you wouldn't find any.

You learned early that value as a person, your worth as a child, had a lot to do with learning how to work. You were often admonished to learn how to work. You were advised that the only alternatives were to starve, steal, or beg, which were not painted as particularly attractive.

Boys were expected to get these values through their heads, or, if necessary, they would be pounded into their heads, along with a few other things. Adults seemed pre-occupied with getting things into our heads, one way or another, pounding being the most popular and effective.

You were typically advised that you had to learn to work if you wanted to keep a job. Our parents seldom talked about us boys going to college and getting into the professions. The gas and telephone companies and the railroad were good jobs. Parents were not ambitious for us. The main thing was to get a good, steady job and bring home a check every week that a family could live on and pay the bills. Paying the monthly bills was mandatory. Living on your check was very important. You could run a charge account at some stores, but those bills had to be paid the first of every month. The first of every month was a very serious time as you tried to make the money stretch.

Most of my friends' mothers didn't work outside the home, except for maybe Sister Rhodes, Sister Oldroyd, Sister Gatenby, who was a nurse, and one or two others. My mother went out cleaning other women's houses for a dollar an hour. She had weekly customers, sometimes working in one house in the morning and another in the afternoon—Mrs. Clark, Mrs. Merrill, Mrs. Duckett, Mrs. Gray.

When she was younger, she worked for a Provo family that had an older daughter who was mad. One day the daughter got a straight-edge razor and was going to cut my mother's throat, but my mother ran out of the house and never went back. My mother laughed when she told the story. The daughter later was committed to the State Hospital. My mother told stories of friends, neighbors, and ward members who were committed. It was not unusual for people to go crazy or insane. Nervous breakdowns were fairly common, especially for women.

My mother loved to tell stories about the people she worked for, their troubles and problems. Money and position didn't make any difference to her. Everybody was human. If somebody had been particularly mean or selfish, she said, "They aren't dead yet." This, I finally understood, meant they still had time to suffer for the misery they caused other people, something my mother firmly believed.

She often sang gospel hymns while she worked. She laughed a great deal. She often said, "You might as well laugh as cry in this old world."

My mother was gone five and six days a week cleaning. We didn't have a phone, so women would call Mrs. Gray, who lived next door, and leave messages for my mother. We didn't have a car, but good cleaning women were hard to find, so that was why the women would come pick up my mother or pay for her taxi.

My mother never tolerated any sass or backtalk. You did as you were told. You might get a penny for candy on occasion, and on rare occasion a nickel for ice cream or a candy bar, and on Saturday a dime for the show, which was your inherited right, but you didn't get paid or get an allowance. Such things were never mentioned. We did not live high on the hog, an expression that took me years to figure out, although I knew it had something to do with eating.

"If you want money, you get out and earn it," my mother said. "Don't come to me for money. I haven't got any for you."

We Sixth Ward boys were expected, as soon as we were old enough to get jobs, to pay for our clothes and other expenses and to hand our mothers a dollar or two if they needed it. We didn't have many clothes, sometimes only one pair of shoes for school, play, and Sunday, with a pair of galoshes to go over them in winter. Washing clothes was a long, trying task, so we did not change clothes often. When you took your Saturday night bath, you put your whole outfit in the dirty clothes and put on clean underwear to go to bed.

Before my mom and dad were divorced, my dad used to give us each a chocolate bought from a wooden barrel at Safeway when he bought the Saturday groceries. It was an anticipated pleasure to fall asleep on Saturday night with a melting chocolate on the tongue. Families always bought the week's groceries on Saturday. The small ward grocery stores let you charge groceries, but Safeway didn't.

After they were divorced, my mom never criticized my dad but said he did the best he could. He was old, blind in one eye, and often out of work.

If your mother sent you to the store and she didn't have any money, she would say to charge it or put it on the bill. This bill had to be paid every month. If a family didn't pay its bill, it couldn't charge any more groceries, which meant you'd starve. You were often told that starving was a possibility under the circumstances, or even starving to death, which was worse.

My mother had no savings or checking account. All the money she had was in her purse. Her purse was very important, the source of all family wealth and something you were sent to get if money was required. If you were sent to the store, you automatically asked if you could have a penny for candy—never a nickel or a dime, only a penny—and you usually could, but sometimes not. Stealing a penny from your mother's purse was a fairly common crime, but never more than a penny.

When things really got tight, Bishop Oldroyd would give my mother a grocery order on the bishop's storehouse. Brother Whitehead, who ran the storehouse, always gave us a piece of candy and told us what good boys we were to help our mother.

When you were old enough, you went evenings to work on the church welfare farm down by the lake to thin and top sugar beets and haul hay. We knew the church had farms, orchards, dairies, and ranches to raise food to give to the members who didn't have any, which was another proof the church was true because it helped keep you from being hungry or even starving to death.

Until we got to Dixon Junior High and were required to shower after gym, we took one bath a week in a bathtub, always on Saturday night in preparation for Sunday. Third West houses didn't often have showers, and sometimes more than one kid used the same bathwater. Hot water was scarce. You always felt the tank behind the kitchen stove to see if there was enough hot water for you and complained bitterly if there wasn't. Getting your share of the hot water was important to your sense of individuality and personal worth. To keep the bathroom free of unpleasant smells, you struck a match from the box on top of the toilet.

A boy was expected to keep his face and hands washed and his hair combed and was often reminded to complete these civilizing tasks, particularly washing behind his ears, before coming to supper, and he could expect to be sent back to the bathroom to try again if the result didn't pass inspection. An obvious sign of his growing maturity was when a boy could lock the bath-room door and take a bath without intrusion or help. However, a brother or a sister was always yelling to hur-ry up because they needed to use the bathroom, so there was really little peace.

The wolf was perpetually at the door, we were just scraping by, or my mother didn't have a dollar in her pocket, which meant we were broke. When I was young-er, I really expected to open the front door and find a wolf lurking there. I didn't know what he was going to do, but I knew it wouldn't be good. I was fully aware of what had happened to two of the three little pigs.

12

Wolfman, Tarzan, a dime and a penny, good guys

THE PARAMOUNT, UINTA, STRAND, PROVO, and the new Academy were the movie houses or picture shows where we found our Saturday heroes — Tom Mix, Tarzan, Hopalong Cassidy, Gene Autry, Randolph Scott, Robin Hood, King Kong, the Lone Ranger and Tonto, who were as real to us as our own parents, the difference between the good guys and the bad guys, between right and wrong, never in doubt. Except we couldn't understand how a hero could be killed in one film and then be alive in another film the next week. We used to talk about how this could happen but received no satisfactory answer. We wanted a dog like Rin-Tin-Tin but not like Lassie, who was too pretty and sentimental and far too smart for any real dog.

Walking home in the early evening, the light fading, we practiced Tarzan's yell, hoping perhaps to call herds of friendly elephants from the backyards or talking gorillas from the trees. Along the wooded Provo River, we searched for vines to swing from and wished crocodiles lurked on the riverbanks so we could save Jane from certain death, although she was a bother at times. We wanted to swim fast and sure like Tarzan and dive from high ledges and limbs, the dives perfect so that you were like an arrow.

We envied Tarzan his loincloth, which he got to wear

all the time, and his big knife, the biggest hunting knife we'd ever seen, for killing animals in deadly hand-to-hand combat. But perhaps most of all we envied Tarzan his yell echoing through the jungle. Tarzan's tree house was the greatest tree house in the world and so much better than anything we had constructed that there was no comparison.

Dracula, the Wolfman, and Frankenstein were real too, helping fill our boys' lives and imaginations with pleasing horror on dark stormy nights. Tight with terror, we watched as Frankenstein was brought to life, the electricity coursing through his body, and then he broke the metal straps to rise and pursue those who had afflicted him.

We knew that Wolfman could be killed only with a silver bullet, and on full-moon foggy nights we watched for his dark figure moving along the Sixth Ward streets, wanting perhaps all the time to be bitten so that we too could change into a wolf, have that power, watch our hands and arms become hairy, look in the bathroom mirror to see our ears grow pointed, our teeth long and sharp, and go out and terrify ward members and school teachers, but perhaps not our mothers, who already had their suspicions.

But we didn't particularly want to become vampires and drink the blood of beautiful girls, their white necks exposed and inviting as they slept. We'd tasted enough blood from nosebleeds and licked enough blood from our own wounded fingers and hands to know that blood wasn't particularly delicious. But we believed in vampires. We knew the only way to kill a vampire was to drive a stake through his heart, which we were perfectly willing to do should the occasion arise. Vampires were not to be trusted. We didn't go to Shirley Temple movies, although a vampire movie with her in it would have been interesting, or seeing what happened after Wolfman bit her.

We envied Robin Hood, who had to be the greatest bow-and-arrow shot in the whole world. Even if his opponent in the archery contest shot a perfect bull's eye right in the center, Robin could split his arrow and win. And we envied him his ability with a sword, his flashing blade driving the foe back against the castle wall, finally to run him through, as he justly deserved. Sherwood Forest had to be the best place in the world to live. Utah didn't have anything remotely like Sherwood with its marvelous giant spreading trees, deep deer-populated glades, and trout-filled brooks.

King Kong was the greatest beast in the world, primordial, huge, able to kill dinosaurs and fifty-foot-long, six-foot-thick snakes, beating their heads against a log, and to break down great high thick gates meant to keep him out. But we regretted his falling for that dumb blonde. He should have been smarter than that; he should have stayed on the island. Even we knew at our tender age that women were trouble, particularly blondes. But at least Kong got one of the fighter planes that came to shoot him off the top of the Empire State Building, snatching it from the sky and crumpling it in his wide hands.

Treasure Island was great, Jim finding all that treasure and shooting the pirate who was climbing up the mast to kill him with a knife. Long John Silver was okay too, even if he was a pirate, because he liked Jim and protected him. Being able to find a treasure like that had to be the greatest thing in the world. We boys all believed we'd find a treasure someday. We deserved to.

We wanted to find Montezuma's treasure, which we believed had to be buried somewhere in the hills around Provo, or perhaps down in the fields or around the lake. Montezuma's faithful followers had to bring it this far north to get it away from Cortez and the rest of the greedy, murdering Spaniards. It was the greatest treasure in the world, even greater than what the Count of Monte Cristo found after being in prison for twenty years, which treasure he richly deserved. That was another really good show.

Dawn Patrol, All Quiet on the Western Front, Gunga Din, and *Four Feathers* were great war movies, the heroes all true and brave without any beautiful women to distract them, fighting to the last, sometimes getting killed themselves but always saving their men, winning the battles, always heroic and splendid, just like we would have been if we'd been lucky enough to fight too. We'd all win the Medal of Honor, but maybe they'd have to give it to our mothers in a big ceremony because we would be dead. And the whole town of Provo would be there and be sad but happy too because we'd been so brave and died for our country, a fate that I, believing wholeheartedly in tragic heroes, liked to imagine.

Then in the late thirties in the Movietone News we saw the black-and-white images of real approaching war — Czechoslovakia, Austria, Poland, and then France and England, the marching armies, the goose-stepping Nazis, the navies, the tanks, the fleets of bombers, and the long lines of American men being drafted. In the evenings we listened, heads bent close to the small radios, to the detailed reports, and then Pearl Harbor happened and President Roosevelt said we would win finally, which we didn't doubt, because you could beat anybody who marched like that. The new war films like *Wake Island, Bataan, Flying Tigers*, and *Manila Calling* convinced us that even if we lost most of the time, we knew we would win somehow finally in the end.

We boys were not afraid. We would gladly have joined

the army if the government would only be reasonable and lower the age requirement to twelve or maybe fourteen. We did not envision that .22 and shotgun shells would be in short supply, along with sugar, butter, and gas. We wanted to be snipers, fighter pilots, tank drivers, commandos, machine gunners, paratroopers, bombardiers.

Even though our parents were perpetually broke, *broke* a talismanic word whenever a boy asked for money, we were still entitled to a dime for the show and a penny for candy for the Saturday matinee. This was our right because at the matinee you saw a cartoon, a serial continued from the previous week, and two new main features, which you already knew about because of the previews last week and because you'd been by at least twice during the week to check the posters and big glossy black-and-white photos just to be sure.

Hurrying, your dime and penny clutched tight in your hand and deep in your pocket so you wouldn't lose it and your life be ruined, you and two or three buddies headed uptown to the Uinta. You paid for your ticket, entered the silver doors, breathed in deep the smell of stale popcorn and worn carpets and upholstery, spent your penny on an all-day sucker or jawbreaker because they lasted longer, and walked down the aisle in the already darkened hall, the previews just about to begin. Letting out a sigh, you settled back in your seat, pulled the darkness in around you, and prepared to enter the other real world about to appear before your eyes.

You stayed as long as you wanted, saw everything over at least twice, because they didn't turn up the lights to empty the house, people coming in all the time. Even though your mother had told you to see the double feature through only once and you had promised, you couldn't force yourself to leave, although you knew the consequences when you got home.

So maybe your mother sent your big brother to come and get you, which the usher would let him do, and you saw him walking up and down the aisle looking for you and you ducked, but then he spotted you and told you mom was mad and you'd better get home right now because you were going to get it, a fact he mentioned with apparent relish. Blinking your eyes, you walked out through the silver doors into the searing, blinding late-afternoon heat and light of the other, less heroic world.

And if your brother didn't come after you and you finally managed to get home on your own, your mother was waiting for you, as you knew she would be.

"Well, young man, I thought I told you to see the movie through only once."

"Aw, Mom, it was so great I—"

"Don't you 'Aw, Mom' me, young man."

And then inevitably you were set to some forbidding task to pay for your transgression, all the joy gone from your Saturday life, your only prospect grim eternal church meetings tomorrow.

13

rubber guns, hand grenades, torture, sparrows, BB guns

RUBBER GUN AND SWORD FIGHTS were essential to our summer lives. We sawed and shaped pistols and rifles from scrap wood, fastened a clothespin to the handle to hold the rubber band cut from inner tubes, and then stretched it along the barrel. We usually tied a knot in the middle of the rubber band to make it hurt more. We scrounged blown inner tubes from the service stations. Made of real rubber, they had a wonderful elasticity, the thinner and smaller the tube the better. Truck tubes were useless.

Russell Madsen, who lived through the block, and his friends, Max Mitchell, Bob Anderson, and Bob Conant, built kayaks, fire-cracker cannons, a diving helmet from a five-gallon can and garden hoses and two tire pumps, blow guns, arrow guns, gas-driven model airplanes, a model submarine that sank and came up, and model square-rigged frigates with deck cannons that actually fired, with which they fought battles on Utah Lake, trying to sink each other. They had shops, were five years older than we were, their accomplishments far beyond us. We envied Russ and his friends for their skills and, later, because they got to fight in the war.

To be properly equipped for battle, you needed two rubber-band pistols or a pistol and a rifle. A rubber band had a killing range of twenty to thirty feet, so you had to be fairly close. The idea was to sneak up on the enemy and blast him at close range. You weren't supposed to shoot for the face, but the back of the head and the neck were okay. A rubber band could sting if your aim was right, the enemy's clothes were tight and thin, and you were close enough. You usually tried to shoot him in the T-shirt, front or back.

A good sword fight was enjoyable. We made our swords from laths, readily available. We sanded and scraped the laths and attached a hand guard. We didn't make a sharp edge or sharp point, though both were possible. Mothers didn't like their sons to come screaming into the house flowing blood from a head wound. We learned early on that we had to get along with our mothers, although at ten and eleven we already understood there was much it was best they didn't know, if you wanted to keep your life pleasurable.

We made our shields from heavy cardboard. Most cardboard was too soft, but if you searched through big uptown store trash bins carefully and long enough, you could find the right material. The shields were fairly long to protect as much of the body as possible. The idea was to whack on your opponent's shield until you got an opening and could jab him in the guts and tell him he was dead, a claim that inevitably started an argument.

"You're crazy. You didn't even touch me."

"Yes, I did. You're just a big liar."

Spears and hand grenades were legal weapons, but not bows and arrows. You could see a spear coming and duck, but not always an arrow. We made bows and arrows but didn't use them in battle. We didn't use rocks either, at least not in close battle. We sometimes got in rock fights, but at reasonably long range so you could see the rock coming and duck. We all had flippers or slingshots and became very accurate with them, particularly when we shot marbles, but we didn't fight with them. Putting out a friend's eye, denting his skull, removing a tooth, knocking him out with a head shot, or opening up a bloody wound were considered serious crimes by our mothers, so we avoided them when possible.

We used flippers for breaking bottles, knocking off rows of cans set on a fence, killing birds if you were really good, and for shattering outbuilding or abandoned-house windows at long range with relative impunity, if you could assess the trajectory. The better shots among us liked to knock out Provo Greenhouse windows. Half a block long, built of small glass panels, the two greenhouses located on Second West just across from the mill-race were tempting targets.

The best material for a hand grenade was the dust from a vacuum cleaner, wrapped in toilet paper and tied with a string. The idea was to hit the enemy on the head so the hand grenade exploded and blinded him temporarily. This was hard, but it could be done. The effect was well worth the effort.

To do battle, we divided up sides, four or five boys to a side, and then decided which army would hide and which would attack. Screaming and yelling, hollering who was dead and who wasn't, running, climbing fences, jumping off the roofs of low sheds, leaping out of bushes, dropping out of trees, we attacked and counterattacked, whacking and jabbing with swords, firing rubber guns, throwing spears, and tossing hand grenades, until all the boys on one side had been slain, and then we started all over again.

We had BB-gun fights, but not in the neighborhood. We saved that for the beaches of Utah Lake. Such fights were only truly fun if clothes didn't lessen the BB's impact and full effect. To see a fleeing foe scream piteously, clasp his bare buttock with both hands, and jump six to eight feet into the air was deeply satisfying.

In the darkest night we never ran naked through the neighborhood. Basic Mormon morality required that a boy keep on his shorts. Even if a boy was pantsed or didn't play strip poker with particular skill, he always got to keep his shorts, day or night. There was a difference between being naked and *stark* naked, because when your mother wanted to emphasize naked she always said stark naked. It was worse to be stark naked, but we didn't know why. We knew that Adam and Eve were just naked in the Garden of Eden, not stark naked—at least nobody ever said they were—which helped make just being naked okay.

We hunted neighborhood sparrows with our BB guns, but usually this was with only two boys together, one to shoot and one to spot. It wasn't a gang activity. Walking under the trees, listening for the friendly chirping, watching for movement, we moved from tree to tree, silent except for whispering. Once a sparrow was spotted, you had to move into position for a clear shot. It was difficult to kill a sparrow on the first shot unless you hit him in the head. Usually the first shot stopped him from flying, and then it took two or three more shots to drop him out of the tree, your spotter telling you every time you hit him.

What you hoped for was for the sparrow to light on a telephone wire, because then you could see him fall when you killed him. Most of the fun was seeing the sparrow fall. You knew you'd hit the sparrow in the head if a drop of velvet blood formed at the end of the beak, proof you were a good shot. Dead sparrows felt warm and very light when you picked them up.

We also trapped sparrows. You needed five bricks,

two for the ends of the trap, two for the sides, and then the brick that fell when the trap was triggered. We used bread crumbs for bait. You tied a string to a stick that held up the brick that closed the trap, ran the string out where you could hide, and then waited for a sparrow to get in the trap. You fixed the bricks so that when the one brick fell it didn't crush the sparrow. You could also set the trap so a sparrow could trigger it by himself, but that took a certain expertise.

For a penny, at Clayton's grocery store you could buy a sulfur firecracker that burned with a long trail of smoke before it exploded. We tied one of these to the captured sparrow, lit it, and then let him loose, the smoke trailing like a burning Japanese Zero or a German Messerschmitt, and then the explosion, and the sparrow fell, sometimes. It was always disappointing when he didn't.

We shot only sparrows, never robins or other song birds, which we knew was wrong somehow, although our parents did not forbid us. Perhaps it was an intuitive knowledge passed down from one generation of boys to another. Having saved the Mormon pioneers from the crickets, seagulls were sacred birds, but they were too big to kill with a BB gun, and you couldn't get close enough anyway.

Tired of fighting or shooting sparrows, we might go to the jungle, a dense stand of box-elder trees behind the Roberts Hotel on University Avenue, to see if anybody was going to be tortured, which was something the older boys did, and we got to watch. The victim was usually one of us younger boys they'd captured or lured to the jungle, or one of their own number who had somehow displeased them, or perhaps some boy from another neighborhood who'd wandered into enemy territory.

The torture was to tie his hands and then tie him to a tree, build a small fire by his feet, assemble the boys in a half-circle, and pee into the fire. The victim, if he wasn't gagged, yelled and screamed, twisting his head from side to side to avoid the deadly fumes. The older boys might untie the limp victim or leave him to untie himself. He knew better than to tell his mother what had happened. He put out the fire usually.

Other forms of torture included hanging a victim with a rope by the neck so that just his toes touched the ground, trapping boys in an underground and throwing in dust and dirt to choke them, bending back fingers but not breaking them, twisting arms behind the back, holding a boy underwater while swimming at the river, and pushing a boy's bare feet next to a bonfire but not really burning them. It was usually older boys torturing younger boys, but your friends might torture you if the circumstances were right and they were in the mood. My brother Rowland had a unique blow called an earthquake that, when delivered with a doubled fist to the back, proved effective.

We favored the Chinese water torture, which required tying the victim down and dripping water on his forehead, one drop at a time from a specially made vessel, to drive him insane and also eventually penetrate his skull. But it took too long, and we didn't have the appropriate vessel, although we tried punching a hole in a tin can. We'd also heard of planting a bamboo shoot on the tied victim's naked stomach. We understood that the fast-growing bamboo grew roots down into the victim's vitals, killing him slowly, painfully. But we didn't have any live bamboo, and, again, it would probably take too long.

One day we built a four-foot high volcano out of clinkers from somebody's coal furnace, lit rags soaked in oil for smoke and flame, and then took turns swinging over it on a rope attached to a high tree limb. Just as Dean

Gray, easily the nicest boy in the ward at the time, swung over the volcano, Rowland threw on a can of gasoline, Dean, badly singed, later emerging through the wall of flame. As anticipated, Sister Gray was not pleased. Dean was handsome and played the piano. I don't know where Rowland got the gas. One can only assume he must have been saving it for the right occasion.

14

oath and law, black sheep, brothers and sisters

WE LIKED BECOMING SCOUTS at twelve. One Scoutmaster, Frank Clayton, owner of Clayton's grocery store, was from Alaska, and he taught us how to cook in Dutch ovens and how to dig holes in the ground, line them with rocks, build a fire in the hole, then put your food in the hole, bury it, and let it cook. We learned how to make fires with flint and steel. Harold B. Jones, who served as Scoutmaster the longest, took Troop 48 to Yellowstone in an old bus we fixed up in Brother Hafen's yard. We boys envied the Hafens because they owned a gold mine in Nevada. The Scouts also went to the Uinta Mountains and on other short camping trips.

We worked hard on advancements, and Tom Oldroyd, Rex Berry, and I earned our Eagle badges at the same time. You started as a Tenderfoot, had to memorize the Scout oath and all the twelve laws perfectly, and tie knots and pass them all off. After that you had to pass all the requirements to become a Second Class, First Class, Star, Life, and then finally Eagle, to which I'd always aspired.

As a deacon and a Boy Scout, in my continuing quest to be good I became serious about the Boy Scout Oath and Law. I believed in being "physically strong," "mentally alert," and "morally straight," although I wasn't quite sure what that last one meant; no Scout leader ever brought it up, and I thought it best not to ask. I strove to be prepared and to do a good turn daily. I read my Scout handbook from cover to cover, sometimes at night under the blankets with a flashlight. I liked to wear my full uniform.

I was particularly enthusiastic about the good turn. When riding my bike around town, I looked for little old ladies to help across the street, and I actually located a few. But mostly I wanted to see a house on fire so I could rush in and rescue somebody, particularly a child, a little girl, and drop unconscious from burns and smoke inhalation after carrying the child to safety. But I was never so fortunate.

When you were twelve, you were ordained a deacon, which meant you could pass the sacrament and collect fast offerings to help the poor, and you were entitled to the ministering of angels. I wasn't quite sure what that meant, but I kept my eyes peeled. You were a deacon until you were fourteen, when the brethren laid their warm hands on your head again and ordained you a teacher. As a teacher you could prepare the bread and water trays for the sacrament and be a ward teacher, which meant you went with a Melchizedek brother to ward families to teach the gospel and see if they were in dire want or need. At sixteen you became a priest and blessed the sacrament, kneeling behind the sacrament table in front of everybody and reading the prayers, and you could baptize people.

After eighteen, you received the Melchizedek Priesthood and were made an elder, and after that a seventy and a high priest when you were old. All the older brethren were high priests. An elder went on a mission for two years to preach the gospel, and when he got back he was supposed to get married within six months or a year and raise a big family so the anxious spirits in heaven could have bodies. An elder blessed the sick and raised them from their beds of affliction, and if he had great faith he could even call people back if they'd just died. He couldn't resurrect people who had been buried, just call them back, but they had to have just died, so he couldn't wait too long. Resurrecting them didn't happen until after the Second Coming, although I wasn't sure why.

I wished we had some man in the Sixth Ward who had been brought back. He would have been a useful person to talk to and ask questions. Given my growing desire to lead a righteous life, I was interested in knowing what the other side was like, and if the righteous received all the rewards the speakers talked about in sacrament meeting, and how big the mansions in heaven actually were. I'd come to believe that keeping the commandments paid off.

But my religious life didn't always go as planned. I was supposed to give a talk in sacrament meeting one evening but fell asleep and didn't make it. I was informed later that Bishop Oldroyd said two or three times during the meeting that Brother Thayer was a faithful young man and would be there, but Brother Thayer didn't make it. I seriously considered never showing up in church again. But when I told my mother, she said, "Such nonsense." This was an expression she often used in reference to me.

My mother, who read tea leaves and went to fortune-tellers, had dreams about dead relatives. She heard voices in the middle of the night or a knocking at the door. She told stories about people she knew who had been called back from death because their mission in this life hadn't been fulfilled. When one of our relatives died, she wondered what kind of reception they got on the other side and who was there to greet them when they went through the veil.

Sometimes dead relatives came back to warn wayward members of the family, called black sheep by my mother, to repent. My mother was always talking about black sheep. There seemed to be a lot of them around. I grew up knowing all about the other side and black sheep. I wondered if there were also gray sheep but determined it probably wouldn't be appropriate to ask.

Members sometimes drifted away from the church. If you stopped going to meetings, stopped paying your tithing, broke the Word of Wisdom, or didn't listen to the warning voice of the prophet and the apostles, you were drifting. Some of my friends drifted as they got older, but some didn't have to drift because they weren't faithful members to begin with. You had to be a faithful member first in order to drift. It was always a danger. Straying from the straight-and-narrow path was perilous to your immortal soul, as was letting go your hold on the iron rod, which, according to the Book of Mormon, was the word of God.

I went over to my friend Dave's house one afternoon, and his mom answered the door after I'd yelled Dave's name a few times. She said she was surprised at me because she thought I was a good boy and didn't smoke.

"I don't smoke." Smoking was a sign you were a real drifter.

"Well, David smokes, and birds of a feather flock together."

What could I say? I didn't smoke real cigarettes, but I did indulge in cedar bark and Indian tobacco, a local weed, which I suppose made me one of the flock, technically. As far as I knew, Dave's mother never mentioned her beliefs to my mom. At least if she did, my mom never nailed me for it. One beer or one cigarette, and your reputation as a faithful Mormon boy was shot, those two indulgences a certain and sure measure of your sinful, wayward life and easily worse than bank robbery.

One thing that kept me from drifting was singing the hymns. I loved to sing hymns. One of my Primary teachers noticed I had a pleasing voice and arranged for me to sing "I Am a Mormon Boy" for our graduation: "A Mormon boy, a Mormon boy, I am a Mormon boy. I might be envied by a king for I am a Mormon boy." I pulled this off successfully, and, glorying in the congratulations, resolved at that moment to be a great singer. And although I sang another solo or two in church, I had a tin ear and found it difficult to stay on pitch, plus I couldn't read music; thus, I soon met disaster. After singing "God Bless America" flat all the way through, I overheard someone say as I walked off the stage, "I wouldn't let him sing to my cow."

Yet, full of faith in my latent ability, I started taking singing lessons from Miss Marguerite Jepperson, the Sixth Ward choir director. Miss Jepperson had about twenty-five cats, with maybe ten or fifteen always sitting on the porch railing when I came for a lesson. Miss Jepperson usually held one or two on her lap, with maybe one lying on the top of the upright piano. After the lesson she would send me to the store to buy two pounds of hamburger with the fifty cents I paid her, which, standing on her front porch, she rolled into balls and tossed to the circling cats. The lessons didn't seem to help much.

In church they always prayed for the servicemen to return safely and keep all the commandments and not be enticed by the sins out in Babylon and become black sheep. The servicemen always wore their uniforms to church when they came back, so you knew they were probably just finishing their basic training or flight school. Jump boots and bloused pants meant they were paratroopers. But then they would be gone to the war, and you knew you probably wouldn't see them until the war was over. We boys envied our older brothers and the other ward members who got to be in the war, like Russ Madsen and his friends.

They were lucky, but four Sixth Warders died in the war. Hugh Brown was shot down over the English Channel, Paul Smith over France, and Earl Callahan over Mindanao. Max Hodson was killed on Luzon. We boys didn't know Hugh, Paul, or Earl, but we knew Max. He was Owen's brother, but he was older, married, and lived in Spanish Fork.

We wanted desperately to fight, earn medals, and be heroes. Through the Movietone News, radio news programs, *Life* magazine, and the good war movies like *Sergeant York*, *Bataan*, *Flying Tigers,* and *Wake Island,* we kept track of the war and all the big bomber raids over Germany and all the battles we were winning in North Africa, Italy, and the Pacific. *Sergeant York* was about World War I, but that was okay; it was still true.

Rowland changed the date on his birth certificate and joined the navy at fifteen, which you weren't supposed to do until you were seventeen. An older boy who delivered Western Union telegrams told me once that he delivered a War Department telegram to a house, and when the woman opened it on the front porch she began to scream. He said he could hear her screaming two blocks away.

In the *Herald* they published the pictures of all the Utah County men who were killed, wounded, or missing in action. Every family that had somebody serving hung in their window a small blue flag with a star in the middle, a flag for every serviceman or servicewoman. Jim Rhodes's two sisters, Maxine and Beulah, were both navy nurses and had big blue capes with red lining. A gold star in the window meant the son or husband had been killed. Riding our bikes through the neighborhood, we looked to see what color the star was. Some families had little lights so you could see their flags at night.

Even during the war we still had ward dances, parties, dinners, plays, and reunions, depending on the season. The ward dinners were always potluck, the whole cultural hall filled with tables heavy with food, each sister bringing her best dish. And you could eat as much as you wanted—potatoes, gravy, vegetables, fried chicken, salads, rolls, jams and jellies, cakes, pies, and homemade ice cream. And nobody cared how many times boys went back for seconds on dessert. The treats at the annual Christmas party were particularly inspiring to continued religious devotion.

All the brothers and sisters visited and talked, laughed, and had a good time, and afterward there was always a program, with members playing musical instruments, singing solos, and doing readings and skits, all to loud applause. The master of ceremonies told jokes on the bishop and the Relief Society president and other members of the ward, some of them slightly scandalous, always to great laughter. We had three-act plays performed on the stage and lots of community singing.

There were no inordinately righteous families in the Sixth Ward who everybody looked up to and followed. Everybody seemed about equally faithful. All the families lived pretty much in the same-sized houses and drove the same kinds of old cars. After the end of the war, quite a few young married couples moved in, the husbands going to BYU on the G.I. Bill, but they were too busy going to school, working, and having babies to worry much about being more righteous than anybody else.

In the summer the whole ward went up Provo Canyon for picnics at Canyon Glen, Vivian Park, or South

Fork. Everybody brought a lunch, and the ward furnished the drinks and the ice cream. There was always a softball game, and horseshoes for the men and older boys, and sack races and relays for the kids, with candy bars as prizes for the winners. The yearly ward reunion brought a lot of former members back to visit, the older members sitting around talking.

So church wasn't all boring for a boy.

15

cardboard towns, fire, durmer, sirens, jobs

ENGAGED IN OUR VARIOUS pleasurable roaming activities,
we boys did not wear or need watches. We told time by
the sun, by how hungry we were, by the Troy Laundry
noon whistle, and by the Heber Creeper coming back in
the afternoon. We were not necessarily expected home
for lunch, probably only a sandwich and a bowl of fruit
anyway, or maybe soup. Our mothers knew that if we
were hungry enough, we'd come home, if only briefly.
A sound we instinctively listened for, in addition to the
Troy whistle, was the wailing siren of an approaching
fire engine, cop car, or ambulance. We longed to see a
house going up in flames or the carnage of a wreck.

A major project on a hot summer day was to build a
cardboard town, a connected group of cardboard huts
maybe a hundred feet square, with various windows,
skylights, doors, and hidden passages. We constructed
our towns in Clowards' vacant lot on the corner of Second South and Second West across from Liddiards'.

Our building materials were the big cardboard boxes
we salvaged from the trash bins behind Sears, Penney,
Dixon-Taylor-Russell, Taylor Brothers, Firmage's, and
the other major stores, all within two or three blocks of
the building site. A line of five or six boys dragging big
boxes along the sidewalk was not an uncommon sight.

No adult ever stopped us or even asked us what we were doing, although we made repeated trips.

We cut the doors and windows with pocket knives, saws, and sneaked butcher knives. You had to be careful using a long-bladed knife because there might be a kid in the next room and you didn't want to run him through, but this never occurred. Once built, a cardboard town with its secret doors, passageways, and rooms was a splendid place for tag, surprise attacks, kidnapping, torture, strip poker, assaults, and smoking. For light in the dark interior, we used candles and sometimes flashlights, if we could sneak one from the house.

After two or three days, we grew tired of the cardboard town, and they sometimes burned, usually in the evening or night when the flames were best seen. Neighbors came out of their houses to watch and smile. There was no danger, unless of course a boy were somehow trapped in a secret torture chamber, but this wasn't likely. One fire department truck came, the quick flames inevitably dying by the time they arrived, but we enjoyed hearing the siren.

Innocent, we always stood in a group, our hands in our pockets or arms folded across our chests. Rolling up their hoses, the firemen were not amused.

"What are you little buggers trying to do, burn down the whole neighborhood? You ought to have your butts kicked."

Or we deserved a damned good licking or a hiding or to be skinned alive. Not just a licking or a hiding or a whipping, but a damned good one. We understood there were grades of lickings. Being skinned alive sounded pretty bad, but we didn't understand how that was done, and we didn't like to think about it too much.

We said nothing. The firemen had no proof. We knew they wouldn't drag us home and tell our mothers to see that we were justly punished. "Little buggers" wasn't so bad; we'd been called worse.

Another way to enjoy fire was to make a gun with two clothes pegs that would launch a lighted match, the lit match arcing out for maybe ten feet. For ammunition we either sneaked a handful of matches from home or chipped in our pennies to buy a box at Clayton's. We shot at each other, trying to set each other ablaze, which wasn't likely, although you might get your hair singed on occasion if you were careless and somebody made a lucky shot.

The main danger was igniting dry weeds and starting a backyard conflagration. Rowland and some of his friends once set a mountain on fire, but not intentionally. The fire just got away from them. We took reasonable care to stamp out any beginning fires or pee on them if there was time or opportunity and enough boys available with sufficient capacity. We were aware that if the weeds and the weathered, dry outbuildings got going, the whole neighborhood might go up in smoke.

As pleasing as that would have been to watch, we knew our mothers wouldn't approve. When there were no fires to put out and the need arose, we tried to write our names on board fences. Unless a boy had an unusual bladder capacity and force and a short given name or nickname, he typically didn't finish.

Matches were important, and not just for match guns. You needed them for lighting necessary fires, seeing in dark places, cutting off the heads to make bombs, for smoking, and for throwing at the sidewalk to see who could light the most in a row. In addition to cedar bark and Indian tobacco—seeds stripped from a dried red weed—we smoked dry, hollow grape stems and rolled newspaper, not real cigarettes, which was against the Word of Wisdom and a sin.

We did, though, strip cigarette butts we found and saved the tobacco in the little cloth Bull Durham sacks with the drawstring, to no particular purpose. Although it was a sin to smoke tobacco, it was comforting to have a sack of real tobacco in your pocket. We also used the sacks for nuggets of fool's gold and other treasures, which we put in our cigar boxes. Every boy under the age of eleven or twelve had a cigar box hidden away in his secret place. You asked for them at stores. Store owners knew that boys were entitled to empty cigar boxes.

Originally the small sack had held tobacco and an attached folder of thin papers so a man could make his own cigarettes. At a nickel a bag, it was the cheapest way to smoke. In the movies, cowboys always rolled their own cigarettes, pulling the string tight on the Bull Durham sack with their teeth. After you rolled the cigarette, you had to lick the paper to make it stick. A boy who smoked real tobacco was called a durmer.

Roving the Sixth Ward neighborhood on summer days, we might stop at Bandley's Car Repair on Second West just off Center Street to stand in the broad entrance, look down the rows of cars on each side, and watch the repairmen pounding out dents in the metal fenders and doors. The pounding wasn't loud, more like tapping, almost gentle, the repairmen using different-sized hammers and hand anvils to shape the metal until the dent was gone and then sanding and polishing. Over each car a suspended light bulb broke the gloom; sometimes a welding torch flared. Often more than one man worked on a car, the men nodding their heads, talking to each other, passing their hands over the metal to test for smoothness. We liked the noise, the metal smells, the dark scene of men working.

Next door was the Central Dairy, the cement floors always washed, the smells clean and milky. Sometimes our mothers sent us to get a gallon of skim milk for a dime, and we got to look into the vats of curds. Roaming, we might stop at the Troy Laundry and through the windows watch the women feed sheets into the big mangle. The smells were always of steam and water and soap. Although we were growing a little older, we still seemed to spend a lot of time standing and looking in through doors and windows.

The Troy Laundry whistle blew every day at noon. You could hear it all over town, so you knew it was noon. If you were late getting home for lunch or something, your mother would ask you if you had heard the whistle and why you didn't pay attention. But time wasn't important for us boys. Not caring about a past or a future, with no memory or anticipation, we lived only in the present moment. Sometimes our mothers sent a brother or sister to seek us out.

"You better get home. Mom's looking for you. And she's mad too. You're going to get it."

"Why? I haven't done anything."

"That's what she's mad about."

"Ah, nuts."

We liked to wander along Center Street looking in the store windows. The most interesting stores were Sears, the sporting goods stores, and Woolworth's and Kress's, the five-and-dime stores, where you could actually buy something for a nickel. Woolworth's was one of the most interesting because when you bought something, the clerk put your money and the sales slip in a canister, attached it to a holder on a wire, pulled a handle, and the canister zipped up a wire to the cashier's desk in an open office on the next floor. The whole store was crisscrossed with wires, canisters coming and going all the time.

We always checked the Strand, Uinta, and Provo movie theaters to see what movies were coming. We stood looking at the big glossy black-and-white action photographs and talked about how good the show would be. We didn't worry much about the Paramount and the new Academy. They were too ritzy for us. The Uinta was the best place for Saturday matinees, comedies, serials, shorts.

Our favorites were Our Gang comedies, the Marx Brothers, the Three Stooges, Frank Buck, Flash Gordon, and Superman. We particularly enjoyed Our Gang because they were a bunch of boys like us. People told me I looked like Alfalfa because my hair stood up in back like his, which I took as a great compliment.

We went to see *Snow White* and *The Wizard of Oz*, even if they were kind of phony. I wondered if Snow White, when the Prince kissed her awake, threw up the poisoned apple first before she went riding off with him into the sunset. It seemed reasonable, but it would have been kind of a mess. I liked Snow White's stepmother.

As the summer afternoon waned, we might wander up to the tabernacle to see who could walk around the ledge without falling off. The ledge was only maybe five feet off the ground, so there was no danger. It was just a matter of seeing who could do it. The ledge around Provo High School was twenty feet off the ground, which was dangerous. I'd seen older boys do short distances, but if you fell you could really break your neck, or an arm or a leg, or maybe both arms and both legs, so you had to be careful. We younger boys were pleased to watch; we didn't try it.

We sometimes went over to Pioneer Park on Fifth West to swing in the swings or go down the slides, but we'd begun to feel too old for that. Under the green pavilions on the north side of the park, old men, some of them unshaven, played checkers and cards at the tables. Others simply sat and talked, smoked, chewed tobacco, or whittled. We walked over to watch them but didn't get too close. They would sometimes turn to look at us but didn't speak. All the benches were filled, the men sitting close together. The smell was musty.

Or in the late afternoon, we might go down to the hobo jungle behind the ice house to talk to the hobos. During the Depression years before the Second World War, hobos were always coming up Third West from the railroad yards to ask for food, an old coat, or a pair of old shoes. Our mothers fed them on the front porch or invited them around to the back. Sometimes the hobos chopped wood or kindling or did some other service for their sandwich and bowl of soup or stew.

"The poor souls," my mother said. "Who knows what sorrows they have to bear or how far they've come."

We knew that hobos wrote in secret symbols on the sidewalks outside homes where people fed them, and although we looked for these writings we never found any.

In the thick stand of willows and box elders, the hobos had fires, with pots of stew and coffee steaming. The spring just behind the ice house furnished water. They were friendly but did not say much to us.

"Hello, boys."

"Hello."

We just watched. Unshaven, their clothes crumpled and dusty, the hobos looked worn, as if they'd come too far. When we went down to the depot to see the trains come roaring through, the wonderful, enormous black Malley steam engines, the biggest machines we'd ever seen in our lives, the big wheels higher than our heads, we saw hobos sitting in the open doors of boxcars or maybe on top. We waved; they waved, but always slowly, sometimes just lifting a weary hand.

What we most liked to see during the war were the

troop trains coming through, the flat cars loaded with trucks, tanks, half-tracks, and artillery. Soldiers always stood at the open half-doors between the cars or sat at the open windows. We waved and they always waved back, leaned forward, shouted at us, sometimes throwing us PX candy bars or gum, both hard to get during the war.

If the train was stopped, the soldiers talked to us, asked us our names, how old we were, if we had older sisters. We asked them where they were from and if they were going to go fight the Germans or the Japanese.

"Hard to say, kid."

They were from faraway places—New York, Georgia, Alabama, Kansas, Connecticut, Oregon, places we'd seen only on maps in school.

We wanted desperately to fly bombers and fighters, drive tanks, operate machine guns and flamethrowers, fire bazookas, be captains of destroyers, be heroic and wonderful in faraway places fighting great battles. Filled with envy, we told them they were lucky.

"Think so, kid?"

"Sure."

"Well, I'd rather be back home. It ain't no party, kid. I can tell you that."

They waved to us as the train pulled out.

16

Siwash Indian, whipping, crazy, glory, guilt, the veil

AFTER A DAY OF ROVING, we always got asked the inevitable questions by our mothers. "So, where have you been all day?"

"Around."

"What have you been up to?"

The expression "up to" suggested we'd been doing something wrong or perhaps even sinful, but boys didn't become incensed. It was a reasonable question, under the circumstances.

"Nothing."

"Nothing? How can you spend the whole day doing nothing?"

"I don't know."

"Well, get your hands washed. Supper's about ready. And comb your hair. You look like a Siwash Indian." I'd seen Sioux, Apache, and other tribes in the movies but never one called Siwash. I assumed they didn't comb their hair or wash their faces very often.

Our mothers didn't ask about any felonies we might have committed, didn't want details, had not been anxious about our welfare. We were home uninjured, hungry, willing to bring in a scuttleful of coal if asked, and neither the cops nor the sheriff had been at the door, so there was no cause for alarm.

When a boy did step out of line, his mom might crack him with a long-handled wooden spoon, scold him, flip the side of his skull with a thimbled finger, threaten to knock his and his brother's heads together if they were both involved, tell him how deeply disappointed she was in him, or maroon him on a kitchen chair for an hour, or assign him some unpleasant task. But real punishment was left to his father upon his return from work, which the offender was left to anticipate, his fear growing as the fated hour of his father's inevitable coming approached. When you were younger you got spanked or paddled, your dad slapping you on the butt with his hand. But as you matured you got a whipping or a licking, involving the use of a willow switch or your dad's belt or razor strap. Even if you escaped punishment, you were told in no uncertain words that you deserved a good licking, sometimes a damned good one, depending on the gravity of the situation.

None of my friends got licked or whipped on a regular basis, no black eyes or bruised faces visible, and in the showers at school no welts on the back or butt. However, a boy might get cussed, cuffed across the side of the head, dragged into the house by an ear, or he might get a good swift kick in the rear end to start him back in the right direction or get him back on track. Parents thought it important that a boy be headed in the right direction or be on track.

If your mother wanted to try guilt, she might say she'd been working like a slave all day or had worked her fingers to the bone, and you might at least show a little appreciation, or she might say you were driving her insane, crazy, or to the State Hospital. We boys believed this was possible. We rode our bikes up Center Street to see the patients screaming and cursing at us from the barred windows, some waving handkerchiefs. Jim

Rhodes's mother worked there as an attendant, and so did my mother at one time, and my grandma and grandpa, and three of my uncles, one of them for thirty years.

They all told stories about the inmates, some of whom could have been moms driven crazy by their hooligan sons. I was never told this, yet I knew it was a possibility. None of my friends really wanted to drive their mothers to the State Hospital, if it could be avoided. We knew that patients sometimes saved containers of urine to pour on attendants and other people they didn't particularly appreciate.

A boy might be told by his mom, a teacher, or some other caring adult that he was headed straight for the State Reform School in Ogden if he didn't change his behavior and eventually to the state pen in Salt Lake City. A boy was always being told to change his behavior, as if he could do that just because he wanted to, as if he had a real choice in the matter.

As boys we were typically not threatened with a horse whipping, being tarred and feathered, or being ridden out of town on a rail. These were punishments reserved for men, so you had to be older. Usually if an offender was tarred and feathered he was also ridden out of town on a rail. I understood the process of pouring warm tar on a man and breaking a feather pillow over his head, although I'd never been privileged to witness it. But I didn't quite know what being ridden on a rail entailed, and I didn't ask. I often heard that certain men ought to be locked up or put behind bars, and I assumed they eventually were.

As Mormon boys we knew that the top degree of glory was the best and the one everybody should aim for. In church the speakers and teachers didn't say much about going to hell and eternal burning, although you could end up in spirit prison for a while until you repented.

You were often warned about the Second Coming, which could happen at any minute because the world was so wicked, but we boys figured we still had plenty of time to give up our sinful ways before that happened. Somehow it just didn't seem likely on a clear summer morning that Jesus was going to arrive and put an end to all our roving and fun.

The worst thing was being cast into outer darkness after you were resurrected, so you'd be with the devil and the third of the hosts of heaven that rebelled against God before the earth was formed and got cast out and didn't have bodies, which seemed pretty bad. You couldn't do much if you didn't have a body, couldn't go fishing or swimming or eat ice cream or Baby Ruth bars or chug a Royal Crown Cola, things we hoped we could continue doing in heaven. Because you'd been born, you weren't among the third that got cast out early, so it was comforting to know you'd made it this far, anyway.

You would be with your family forever after you died, but my mother said she knew women, some of them not divorced, who preferred not having to live with their husbands all through eternity. This life was plenty long enough under the circumstances, and they hoped the Good Lord would take that into consideration.

I once asked my mother if there were creeks, rivers, and lakes in heaven, because if there weren't and I couldn't go fishing, I wasn't really interested.

She said, "Don't talk such nonsense."

But it wasn't nonsense to me. I was serious.

My friends and I always had the feeling of being watched, with all the Sixth Ward resident adults knowing who we were and what we were doing, unless we were particularly wary. Because most of us went to church and were taught in classes by the adults, mostly the sisters, and gave two-and-a-half-minute talks in Sunday School in front of the whole ward, and were Scouts, our faces and names were public knowledge, our parentage known. So sometimes we grew wary, never knowing when we got home what act of violence or destruction had been reported ahead of us and what dire consequences awaited.

The typical greeting under difficult circumstances was, "Well, what have you been up to this time? And don't you lie to me, young man. Sister Menlove talked to me about your behavior." So you knew you were had and might as well come clean, because your mom would know that you were lying anyway, of course.

It was worse if your family had a phone, which we didn't, because then all a sister had to do to nail you was phone, and it was always the sisters who called our mothers, not the brothers, who perhaps believed less in our perfectability. When we became Aaronic Priesthood bearers and Boy Scouts, it was expected, at least theoretically, that our behavior would improve. You were, particularly as a priest at age sixteen, expected to be worthy to administer the sacrament, this worthiness becoming something of a concern because boys that age were capable of more serious sins we younger boys had begun to hear rumors about.

I feared that Bishop Oldroyd, in a revelatory moment—for bishops were entitled to revelation and were thus to be feared—would suddenly stand up as I or one of my priest friends knelt to say the sacrament prayer and say, "Stop! You are an ardent sinner and not worthy to bless the sacrament! Come with me to my office. You must repent!" And, knowing this to be true, although not privy to which specific trespass had been revealed, you would follow obediently, the ward silent but unsurprised, our mothers shaking their weary heads. But, unlikely as it may seem, this never happened.

Priesthood meeting and Sunday School weren't so
bad because you got to go to class with your friends, and
fast and testimony meeting the first Sunday of every
month wasn't so bad either. Ward members, who'd been
fasting to give the cost of two meals to the poor, stood to
bear their testimonies and say they knew the church was
the only true church on the whole earth. They sometimes
cried, or talked about revelations they'd had, or visits
from the dead, or prophesied, or described their terrible
sicknesses or tragedies and how they'd been spared, or
how they'd gotten pregnant finally, so it was pretty interesting sometimes.

But the two-hour-long regular sacrament meetings
were pretty boring. We boys couldn't possibly understand the speakers. I used to sit and look up at the three
big paintings at the front of the chapel and wonder what
Joseph Smith felt like kneeling out under the trees in the
Sacred Grove seeing God and Jesus and being told to
start a new church.

I wondered if I would ever see a vision like that. None
of my friends ever mentioned wondering about having a
vision or even wanting one. Of course, we were still too
young. And then the Angel Moroni appeared to Joseph
Smith what seemed like at least a dozen times to tell him
how to dig up the gold plates and translate the Book of
Mormon. I used to wonder sometimes what it felt like to
talk to an angel and what you said to him and what kind
of questions you asked about heaven.

Sunday you wore your Sunday shirt and pants and
your polished shoes. It was important for a boy to polish his shoes for Sunday so that he might seem less of a
little heathen, a term often applied to boys. If you didn't
have any shoe polish, you could use milk or soot from
under the stove lid. It was particularly important to stay
clean on Sunday to prove that it was possible; you got

reminded a lot in church that your spirit needed a clean body to stay in, implying that if you were dirty all the time, your spirit would suddenly leave and you'd fall over dead.

Monday morning you put on your clean shirt and Levi's for school or summer play. Our mothers often warned us to keep our clothes clean and not to tear them or wear them out because she and your dad weren't made of money and did you think money grew on trees, which we never thought, but we kept our eyes peeled. It was particularly serious to wear out your shoes, because they were expensive, and my dad always cussed when my mother sent us up to him to buy us new shoes. He said we needed shoes made out of cast iron. Fortunately, shoes could be half-soled and heeled at Kelsch's Shoe Repair or Sam the Shoe Man. Or sometimes fathers did that themselves.

Sunday was the big meal of the week—chicken or roast, mashed potatoes and gravy, carrots or cabbage or squash or turnips or canned peas or beans and home-made bread. For dessert there was cobbler, pie, or pudding, or perhaps just a bowl of bottled fruit. Sunday breakfast might be special, pancakes or waffles or bacon and eggs, but during the week we ate Corn Flakes or Wheaties, and in the winter hot Cream of Wheat or oat-meal, called mush, which we were told would stick to our ribs, and it usually did. Weekday summer lunch, if you were home to eat it, was a sandwich and a bowl of fruit, and when we were in school, lunch was a sandwich in a paper sack or lidded Rex Lard can.

Because of the Depression, most families didn't have the money to send their sons on missions, so there wasn't much talk about missionary work in church meetings. And then during the war all the men either enlisted or got drafted, so they didn't go then either. Boys didn't grow up thinking much about being missionaries; we thought about being drafted or joining the army, if we were lucky and the war lasted long enough.

To go to church meant going to meetings, but to go over to the church meant going to the meetinghouse. But the church could also mean just the chapel or the whole Mormon church. Boys didn't say The Church of Jesus Christ of Latter-day Saints or LDS Church or even Mormon church; we just said church or the church because everybody knew which church you meant.

We didn't think much about what being a Mormon meant. It was just something we were; we didn't talk about it, except that it was the one and only true church. We didn't know about other churches; we had never seen church buildings other than Mormon churches, except the Catholic church on Fifth West. Everybody we knew was Mormon.

Summer sacrament meetings weren't so bad as the rest of the year because they had to open the high, narrow windows on both sides for air, and four or five hornets always came flying in. And you could watch them zooming back and forth making ward members duck. You always hoped somebody would get stung and let out a scream and maybe even swear and take off out of the meeting, maybe a bald-headed man stung on the head, but it never happened, unfortunately. Members, especially the heavy-set sisters, sat fanning themselves with their free Berg Mortuary fans, with a picture of Jesus on one side and BERG MORTUARY printed in big black letters on the other side.

Complaining about how boring sacrament meeting was didn't do much good. Boys were to be seen and not heard, as our mothers so often reminded us.

We believed everything we were told and taught. We were Mormon boys, members of the only true church in the whole world, Mormonism seeping into our blood and bones without our even knowing it. But it was possible to question the faith. At Owen Hodson's funeral Bishop Oldroyd said that Owen was needed up in heaven because he was so prompt and they needed a messenger boy to carry messages. Sitting on the front row, I knew that Owen wasn't any prompter than any of the rest of us, so I had my doubts about that being a good reason why he had to get shot. I didn't forsake my Mormonism because of this insight, but it was perhaps the beginning of a questioning mind.

17

sewer, the Crusher, fetuses, naked, rafts, clay

BY THE TIME WE WERE twelve and thirteen, beginning the
seventh grade at the Dixon and new Boy Scouts and
deacons, we boys needed more room. The Sixth Ward
neighborhood wasn't big enough, our activities there
had become somewhat childish, our lives more serious.
We needed to go out into the world, look at the other
side of the moon—the fields, river, lake, and mountains,
all at easy distance from our homes if we were willing to
walk, ride our bikes, or thumb a ride, because we knew
none of our parents were going to take us anywhere.

We never gave the distance a thought. We walked
from Third West and Third South to the mouth of Slate
Canyon, hiked up Slate and across the backs of two
mountains to Rock Canyon and down, and then walked
home, covering maybe ten miles. Easy.

If we were walking along a road, we always thumbed.
Three or four or five boys together didn't often get a ride,
but sometimes we did, in the back of a pickup maybe.
Our parents never told us not to thumb rides. It was a lot
easier for just two boys to get a ride, particularly if you
were carrying a fishing pole. Men liked to pick us up and
talk about fishing when they were kids.

My father had a wonderful split-bamboo fishing rod
that he didn't use and that I coveted. One day when we

were living on Eleventh West and Third South, I came home from school and he told me that my mother and Rowland, Bob, and Marlene had gone to my Grandmother Thatcher's and wouldn't be back. He said if I would stay with him, he would give me the fishing pole. As much as I wanted the pole, I decided to go find my mother. Walking away, I looked back to see my father standing in the doorway.

Our bikes were precious to us. Because of the Depression and later the war, it was a lucky boy who owned a good bike. Balloon-tired, heavy, one-geared, they were slow but steady. We learned to take the gears apart for cleaning, oiling, and repair, replace damaged chain links, and fix flat tires, puncture weed a curse on the land. We took off the fenders for speed, turned up the handlebars for a better grip. We often rode double, the passenger sitting on the crossbar or the handlebars. It was an unhappy boy whose bike was broken or stolen, the loss terrible because you were marooned, left behind by your friends unless, filled with charity, somebody rode you double.

We longed to be sixteen and old enough to hunt deer, drive, and own a Model A Ford and go wherever and whenever we wanted. Virtually every boy wanted to own a Model A. They were the best cars. Girls liked boys with Model As, and they were good for deer hunting because they were so high-centered. A boy could tear down the engine in his own backyard and do all the repairs; a Model A wasn't expensive.

Older and more wide ranging, we rode our bikes up to Temple Hill to wander through the four buildings on the upper BYU Campus—Maeser, Grant, Joseph Smith, and Brimhall. The Brimhall was the most interesting, smelling strangely of laboratories. The walled-off corner of one room held snakes—including rattlesnakes—lizards, and Gila monsters. We liked it when the rattlers buzzed. We thought the worst death would be to fall into a pit of rattlers. In *Gunga Din* the captured native rebel leader jumped into a cobra pit in the temple so his men would know how brave he was and would fight harder.

In one room of the Brimhall Building was a high shelf of large bottles holding human fetuses arranged in various stages of development. Hushed, we looked up at these a long time. We knew this was serious, important, and instructional, but we didn't know exactly why. We knew women got pregnant somehow and had babies, and this was what the babies looked like before they were born, but you had to have a spirit inside of you to stay alive, which these didn't. It was very important to keep your spirit inside you and not let it get away.

The doors to the rooms were always open. The building seemed almost empty; because of the war, there were few students. If a professor came by, he was not suspicious. He said hello. We were treated not as the hooligans we were but as fellow seekers after knowledge. The lower campus had a big room with dinosaur skeletons and a diorama with a tiger and a crocodile, but they weren't as interesting as the rattler pit and the shelf of bottled fetuses.

Older now, we stopped swimming in the public North Park pool in the cold, chlorinated water, where you had to wear trunks and the lifeguard was always hollering and blowing his whistle. We preferred swimming naked in the river. Our favorite hole was the Crusher, where a big dragline took out rocks to crush for aggregate. Our older brothers and our fathers, if they grew up in Provo, had swum there, so it was a natural thing to do, as if kept in some perpetual and general boys' memory.

We didn't think about swimming naked as wrong or bad, and we called it swimming naked or bare-assed or buck-naked because that's what we did, but never stark naked because that was something special only our mothers understood. We all lived in one-bathroom houses, some families with six or eight children, so privacy, especially for children, wasn't a real issue. We were required to shower after gym in junior high school and high school. And at the Deseret Gym pool in Salt Lake, where the Scouts went in winter to swim sometimes, you didn't wear trunks. So swimming without trunks was just natural, a kind of primitive freedom. We didn't think or talk about it. It was just something boys did when they had a chance.

Forty yards wide, maybe fifty long, fifteen to twenty feet deep, the Crusher was the best swimming hole on the lower river. That low in the valley, most of the river water was taken off in irrigation canals, but enough flowed in and out to keep the Crusher fresh, the water pleasant. We swam and swam, stayed in the water, dived, wrestled, played tag, had water fights, and then, when we tired, floated on the logs that had come down with the spring high water and gotten caught. We fought for the best logs, pushing each other off, tipping the logs, until finally maybe two or three of us floated on one log.

Absorbing the heat, paddling just enough to stay out in the middle, we lay facedown, our hands in the water, our bodies having burned and peeled so often that we were as brown as Indians. Lying forward, you wrapped your arms around the log, and, nose touching the water, looked down into the depths. Carp, suckers, minnows, and trout swam there. Slipping off the log, we sank down to be with them, tried to be a fish. Or, on shore, we found a big rock, twenty or twenty-five pounds, breathed hard to fill our blood with oxygen, took a deep breath, walked into the water, and tried to stay on the bottom to be with the fish.

If we had a new boy with us, perhaps somebody's visiting cousin or a new move-in or a kid we'd just met swimming that day, we sat in a circle in the lotus position and smoked cedar-bark cigars, made out of bark stripped from fence posts and wrapped in newspaper, the cigars big and loose. We lit these and smoked them carefully, never inhaling because the acrid smoke was like vaporized sulfuric acid. However, we encouraged the new boy to breathe in deep and fast.

"Go ahead, try it — it's great. You'll really like it. Just suck in as much air as you can. Go ahead. You got to do it fast."

Our hope was that the cigar would burst into flame and that, his lungs seared, choking, he would drop it into his naked lap. Then, in agony, gasping for his last breath, his eyes half-blinded with tears, he'd run, jump into the Crusher, and try to drown himself to end the suffering.

Another activity in the circled lotus position was to sit silent and attentive in a patch of sand, pee on the sand, and mold a ball. The first boy to laugh, giggle, or speak received the full barrage during his desperate flight for the river. This pastime was called piss-ball silence.

If a boy came down who couldn't swim, who hung back, the older boys grabbed him by the feet and hands, carried him screaming and yelling that he would drown and that his mother didn't want him to get wet, and, swinging him three times, threw him in. Then they lobbed big rocks at him, not trying to hit him but just keeping him out in the deep water, until in his thrashing he was suddenly doing the doggy paddle and staying afloat.

In spite of the obvious benefit of learning to swim, these young boys had unkind things to say to the older boys, sometimes even swearing at them. If a boy went under twice, somebody jumped in after him. We all knew that if you went under for the third time you drowned, and nobody particularly wanted that to happen.

In the late afternoon, the older boys, who had been

working in the fruit orchards, came down to cool their hot, aching, tired bodies. Tall, more muscled, heavier, arrogant, like cave men in the way they moved their arms and legs, they flung themselves into the water. They were different than we were. We looked at them, saw the differences, the obvious maleness, sexuality, the heavy fertility, and wondered about ourselves, wondered if we would ever be like that, would ever find, as rumored, girls in our dreams. But we said nothing to each other. These things we did not talk about in much detail or insight, a beginning sense of that mystery creeping into our flesh and bones.

Going home, when we put on our Levi's that had been lying in the sun for five or six hours on the rocks, we had to be careful not to singe ourselves with the hot copper rivets, keeping them away from our flesh and vitals. Along the road we stopped to pick fruit from available front-yard trees—cherries, apples, peaches, apricots—all in season, sometimes the householders rushing out to shout us away and threatening us with the police and other dire consequences. But we did not consider ourselves thieves. We were hungry and entitled to what the land provided.

Sometimes at night, if our bikes didn't have flat tires and if we hadn't been swimming that day, two or three of us rode our bikes down to the Crusher to swim in the darkness, building up the dying bonfire. We floated mostly, looked up at the stars and moon, or lay on logs, paddled them out to the center and lay there still, quiet, wondering, our bodies one with the log, water, and dark air.

One night a fly fisherman came down to fish where the river entered the hole. He hooked a big trout, the trout jumping and splashing back into the water. After the fisherman landed it, the three of us walked across the white rocks to see it. The fisherman let us hold it, lift it. Heavy in our hands, it was maybe three or four pounds, a beautiful big German brown, gold and gleaming in the moonlight.

Later we stood in front of the fire, the flames reflecting off our shining wet bodies, the fire's heat comfortable even on a summer night, and talked of the big trout and how it felt to hold him. We longed to catch such a trout.

Some days we followed the river all the way to Utah Lake, staying in the band of willows and trees, following the trail until we came to the irrigated, planted fields west of the Geneva Road, but we didn't often do this. Usually we walked or we rode our bikes down Center Street to the overpass and then down the road to the lake.

Professional seiners caught carp in the lake and kept them in big wooden traps in the river to clean out in the fresher water. Across the street from the Dixon Junior High School, they kept carp in a big ditch for the same purpose. Walking along the bank, we saw hundreds, maybe thousands, of swimming carp coming clean.

Big wooden boxes of gutted, iced carp sat on carts at the Denver and Rio Grande station for shipment somewhere. As boys we looked at the carp and wondered where they were going and who would want to eat them. The carp seiners gutted their carp at the mouth of the river. The wind blew the inflated bladders up the river, where we sank them with our BB guns. You had to be a good shot.

Because of the drought, the lake was low, the sandy beaches fifty or a hundred yards wide before edging into the murky gray water. We built sand castles and fought wars to knock each other's castles down. You stood behind your castle and lobbed sand balls to knock down the turrets and walls, finally running and jumping on the castles to smash them flat.

We gathered driftwood to make rafts, brought hammers, nails, and wire for that purpose. The raft finished, a sail mounted, a flag attached, we pushed it as far out into the lake as possible and then prayed for a storm so we could ride the waves, sail across the lake. Storms could come very suddenly over the west mountains, making waves big enough to swamp a small boat. We knew that every year fishermen's and duck hunters' boats sank, and they had to be rescued or they drowned, their bodies dragged for by the sheriff with big three-pronged hooks. We did not fear for our lives. We sought adventure.

If we were close to the road, we wore trunks, but if we rode our bikes through the tamarack for half a mile, careful to avoid the puncture weed, we didn't. As we ran down the long beaches, shouting, yelling, wrestling, our freedom from adults and from their world was total. We molded balls from the ledges of clay for wars. We painted our hair, faces, and bodies with the bluish clay so that we were unrecognizable, even to each other, and cut spears from the willows, so that we had weapons, and fastened our T-shirts into loincloths. Running, throwing our spears at imagined enemies and at each other, we fought bravely and then danced in victory around our fires, the drying clay turning our bodies white.

We hunted carp in the shallow water, clubbing, spearing them, shooting them with arrows. If it was near the Fourth of July and we had silver salutes and cherry bombs, and a carp was still alive, we put one in its mouth and let it go. We waited for the explosion, cheered when the water erupted, knew that we had sunk a German sub. Carp were trash fish and not to be highly regarded.

The mouth of the Provo sewer, mixed with the creosote from the creosote plant and the effluvium from Kuhni's animal byproducts operation, was perhaps a half-mile away from our beach. But we did not think about disease, contagion, filth. I never knew of any boy becoming sick or suffering from any kind of infection. Richard Tucker cut his foot badly on a broken beer bottle when he jumped off the old Sho-Boat into the river. A painter who was working on the boat advised him to stick his foot in a can of turpentine, which he did and then wrapped the offending member in an old rag and rode his bike home, without an obvious or lasting ill effect.

We sometimes brought an empty Spry can and carrots, potatoes, and onions to cook a stew or we made forbidden coffee, our water coming from an artesian well. We did not bring bowls or spoons but ate from the can with our fingers.

Sitting around our fire, we talked more—about life, about things, about school. Someday if we lived long enough we would be in high school and then be drafted and in the war, if it lasted long enough, which we hoped it would. It would be a bitter disappointment if it didn't.

18

pioneers, grizzly bears, Indian princess, Boozer, temples

BOYS KNEW ABOUT the Mormon pioneers. Pioneers were important. We heard lots of Sunday School, Primary, and priesthood lessons and sacrament meeting talks about pioneers and how they crossed the plains in covered wagons to flee Babylon and reach safe Zion in the tops of the Rocky Mountains, where they could live their religion. We knew all about the pioneers' courage and faith and how many died coming in their covered wagons. And how they had to fight the Indians, and a lot of them pulled handcarts because they didn't have covered wagons, and some got caught in an early Wyoming blizzard and froze to death.

Pioneer Day, the twenty-fourth of July, the day the Prophet Brigham Young and the first pioneers entered Salt Lake Valley, was a state holiday, and Salt Lake City always had a big parade and celebration, but Provo didn't. We had our parade on the Fourth of July, and the wards made a lot of the floats. They had a carnival, so if you had the money, you could go on the Ferris wheel, merry-go-round, tilt-a-whirl, giant hammer, and walk around drinking pop, eating cotton candy and hamburgers and hot dogs, the air full of the wonderful smell of frying hamburgers every time you passed a hamburger stand.

In sacrament meeting the week of July twenty-fourth, we sang hymns about the pioneers and heard stories about how much courage and faith it took to cross the plains and how they were an example to all of us, because we should be that way too—"Come, Come, Ye Saints," "Zion Stands With Hills Surrounded," "Israel, Israel, God Is Calling," "Let Us All Press On," "Ye Elders of Israel"—"O Babylon, O Babylon, we bid thee farewell; we're going to the mountains of Ephraim to dwell." My Grandfather and Grandmother Thatcher weren't pioneers, although they had ten children, which would have partly qualified them. Pioneers had big families. My father wasn't a Mormon, so I didn't have any pioneer ancestors on that side either.

In sacrament meeting an old brother with a long white beard used to sit in the corner and fall asleep, and we boys all knew he was a pioneer, although no one ever said he was, and we never asked him. Dave Nelson's family lived in a pioneer house made of adobe brick, and there were other old pioneer houses around and lots of old barns, sheds, and other outbuildings in the centers of the blocks that looked like the pioneers had built them.

Our Sunday School class went to Salt Lake City to Temple Square to see the building where the prophet and apostles had their offices, the tabernacle, the temple, all the statues, and the seagull monument that showed the seagulls saving the pioneer crops from the crickets. We saw the Prophet Brigham Young's houses. We knew that Brigham Young had a lot of wives and a lot of kids, which was okay with us if that's what he wanted. The most interesting thing was when we went into the tabernacle and we stood at one end and somebody dropped a pin at the other end and you could hear it, an example of what great architects and builders the pioneers were when it came to acoustics. We knew that it took forty years to build the temple, to us a long time.

We knew also that in the temple you did work for the dead if they weren't members. You had to search out all your relatives all the way back to Adam. If they weren't members you made them members, got baptized for them, and did other things, ordinances that they could accept or reject, which seemed fair. But they couldn't get out of spirit prison until they repented and somebody got baptized for them.

Before you were born, you were an intelligence or something, and then you had a spirit body made by God, and then you came to earth to have a physical body, and you had your free agency so you could make choices to prove if you wanted to be good or bad and live with Heavenly Father or the devil after you died. The devil and all his followers were jealous of people on earth with bodies and were always trying to get into them and tempt people to be bad like them, so you had to be careful.

Because all my friends' families were Mormon, some of them must have had pioneer ancestors, but it wasn't something they bragged about or thought was particularly important. In their homes I saw no pictures of pioneers hanging on the walls. The pioneers built the Provo Tabernacle where you had to go to the boring stake conference meetings, one speaker after another for two hours in the morning and three hours in the afternoon sometimes, with apostles coming down from Salt Lake to preach long sermons about repentance, tithing, the Second Coming, the Word of Wisdom, the Prophet Joseph Smith, faith, and the wonderful, heroic, long-suffering pioneers, who always kept the commandments. The tabernacle had an unrailed horseshoe balcony. I watched faithfully, hoping somebody would fall off and crash on top of somebody down below, but this never happened.

We boys knew that when the first pioneers came into Utah Valley, it had been full of buffalo, deer, elk, grizzly bears, and mountain lions, the rivers, creeks, and lakes full of fish, and we wished it were still that way. And we wished the pioneers hadn't killed off the game, especially grizzly bears, which were dangerous, and you could prove how brave you were by killing one. And we regretted that the Indians were all gone too, because we wanted to fight them or become blood brothers and live with them.

One of our regrets as boys was that Utah Lake was not still full of trout. We'd heard stories about how, when the Mormon pioneers arrived, it had been deep, clear, and full of big trout, a fisherman's paradise. But the pioneers had overfished the lake, used nets and hauled farm wagons full of trout to Salt Lake to sell. They also dammed the creeks and rivers for irrigation water, so the trout couldn't spawn. The pioneers planted carp, and all the towns dumped their sewage into the lake. Although we knew how brave the pioneers had been, we still held them responsible for ruining the fishing. We wanted the lake to be crystal clear and teeming with big trout.

The only fish that came up the river to spawn were suckers every spring, thousands of suckers, the bottoms of the holes black with suckers. To snag them, we used ten-foot-long bamboo poles with number-two hooks twisted in series to four feet of wire and tied to the end of the pole with heavy twine. Men and boys lined the river jerking the snagging rigs through the holes, sometimes throwing two or three suckers up on the bank at one time. It was all legal, fishermen taking home their catch in gunnysacks. It was fun, never knowing how many suckers you'd snag at one time, but suckers weren't trout.

Some of my friends' fathers who fished and hunted told us stories their fathers had told them about the wonderful fishing and hunting they'd had when they were young, and it made us jealous, but two generations was about as far back as our interest in pioneer history went. We knew that market hunters used to kill hundreds and hundreds of ducks on Utah Lake to sell. There was no limit, and you didn't need a license.

We knew that a beautiful Indian princess had jumped off Squaw Peak because her father wouldn't let her marry the Indian brave she loved, which we thought he probably should have. If you looked at the top of Mount Timpanogos just right, you could see the outline of another Indian princess along the top, but we knew it was too big to be a real princess. It was just something you could see.

We knew there had been Indian wars but didn't know too much about the details, a lack we regretted because it would have made Provo more interesting. We knew vaguely that the pioneers had fought Indians in Rock and Provo Canyons and along the Provo River. Some Indians had been killed in a running battle out on frozen Utah Lake one winter, and a doctor, who was out duck hunting, cut off the Indians' heads to send to a museum.

Once, pioneers killed an Indian brave, cut him open, filled him with rocks, and sank his body in the river, and some other Indians found his body, and that started one of the wars. The first pioneers coming into Utah Valley built a fort by the river and put a cannon in the center of the fort on a raised platform. One day the cannon blew up, killing one man and blowing off another man's hand, which lit on a cabin doorstep.

Also, there was a man who had murdered somebody and was found guilty and condemned to be executed, who sold his body to a doctor for a small sack of candy.

Just before they stood him up against a wall and shot him, he was eating the candy. The building was torn down, so even if we had known all about him and why he liked candy so much and why the doctor wanted his body, we couldn't have gone to look for bullet holes in the brick and maybe faded bloodstains.

And there was once even a pool-hall owner who kept a black bear named Boozer chained to the back door. Boozer liked to drink beer, but he got away and they shot him. My mother called men who drank boozers. If she said a man was nothing but a boozer, that meant he was pretty bad.

19

starvation, peaches, hot water, rice pudding

COMING HOME FROM PLAY in the summer or school in September, you expected to find your mother and maybe a neighbor or aunt canning cherries, apples, tomatoes, corn, pears, peaches, or apricots, maybe two or three bushels of fruit sitting on the kitchen floor. A boy might be sent to get more bottles from the fruit room or cellar and maybe wash them, being sure to get them good and clean before they were scalded. But he didn't actually participate in the peeling, pitting, and cutting, although he would be told to carry out the peelings to the trash or to the chickens or perhaps stand and stir a pot of chili so it wouldn't burn, all this done on a coal stove, the kitchen hot, humid, and full of the smell of ripe, peeled, and cooking fruit. Some families raised their own fruit and vegetables, but most of it was bought at the Orem produce stands out on Highway 89.

And this went on until late September, every fruit and vegetable in its season, cherries first and then apricots and peaches and pears, with corn and other vegetables having their turn. You came home from school or woke in the morning to find the kitchen counter lined with shining filled bottles that you would be expected to carry to storage, sternly warned not to take too many bottles at a time and not to drop any at the peril of your life. All the empty bottles were filled and returned to the shelves until they were needed for lunch, supper, or a snack.

The kitchen was always hot from the heat of the coal stove, your mother slaving over a hot stove, as she might remind you if you complained of too little time to play. The stove was always lit during the day. It was a crime to let the fire go out. In the winter you might heat only the kitchen, the whole family gathered there close to the stove, the warmth comforting and necessary. You were reluctant to leave the warm stove to go to bed in an ice-cold bedroom. Another worry was frozen pipes once the fire died. On especially cold nights, you turned the kitchen tap on a little to keep the water running so the pipes wouldn't freeze. Frozen pipes were serious, and if they didn't break your dad had to get his blow torch, crawl under the house, and thaw them out.

"Well, we won't starve this winter, will we?" Your mother would say this standing proud, looking at her shelves of work, perhaps your father standing with her. It was important not to starve. You were often warned about the possibility, the threat making boys apprehensive, because it was somehow as if we would starve first, given our ravenous appetites, and perhaps be the cause of the rest of the family starving.

But against this possibility the church taught that every family was supposed to have a year's supply of food, fuel, and clothes and avoid debt. So your parents bought their winter supply of flour, sugar, beans, and rice and filled the coal shed with tons of coal, so there would be both food and heat as the winter came on. So you were comforted, somewhat. We were accused of having hollow legs, eating day and night, stuffing ourselves, always being hungry, growing like weeds, having eyes bigger than our stomachs, all indicating how carefully we needed to be watched.

Our houses were full of the smells of ironing, washing, cooking, canning, cleaning, and baking. Once or twice a week, a boy coming through the door would smell baking bread, wonderful bread, the brown, crusty, heavy loaves lying on the counter in a row cooling. Boys were allowed to eat bread, even invited to cut thick warm slices and spread them with butter or margarine and jam or jelly, and then told to go outside to eat it and not to drip jam all over the floor. The margarine came in white pound blocks that you had to mix with the little envelope of yellow coloring to make it look like butter, but it didn't taste as rich and good.

Suppers were simple, often one-dish affairs — macaroni and cheese, stew, soup, rice pudding, beans and ham hock, chili, hash, and Sunday leftovers on Monday. A boy couldn't expect dessert during the week, although he might strike it lucky. All desserts were pretty much from scratch, except for some pudding mixes. A dish of canned fruit was considered a kind of dessert, but nothing special. My mother wasn't big on cakes and cookies, but she made wonderful pies — apple, cherry, lemon, custard, and raisin, and for Christmas and Thanksgiving pumpkin and mince meat.

Coming home from play or from the Franklin or Dixon fainting and gaunt with hunger, you were told to stop complaining, wait for supper, and get yourself a slice of bread and jam and perhaps a bowl of fruit if you were at death's door. At the table you ate what was put in front of you, or, if you preferred to, you could starve. My mother could never tolerate a complainer or a whiner.

"Better where there's none," she would say, which took me a while to understand. Or if you said something wasn't done, she'd say, "Look done to it." I never did figure out that one. Some boys' mothers reminded them of all the starving little boys and girls in China to make them more appreciative, but my mother never did that.

If you had a baby brother or sister, he or she sat in a high chair and was fed from the table, your mother mashing the food with her fork to make it palatable, or perhaps chewing it herself first and putting it into the baby's mouth.

Except for the few mothers who had jobs outside the home, the neighborhood mothers spent their days cleaning the house, doing the washing and ironing, cooking, taking care of babies and sick kids and aging parents, baking bread, sewing and repairing clothes, darning socks, and, in the summer and early fall, canning or putting up fruit and vegetables and making jams and jellies.

"What lives we beggars lead," was something my mother used to say on occasion.

I agreed. Wash day was always a burden for a boy. Before he went out to play or to school, he had to fill the washer and the two rinse tubs with water a bucketful at a time from the kitchen sink, and then later he had to empty them and wash them out. On the radio he heard repeatedly that Tide was in, dirt was out, so he knew that was the best soap to use. Fels Naptha was another good soap. They warned repeatedly about the terrible consequences of tattletale gray in a washing hanging on the clothesline for all the neighborhood wives to see. A boy didn't exactly know what tattletale gray was, but he knew it was bad.

A boy might have to stand and hand his mother clothes pegs as she hung out the wash and help her fold the fresh, clean-smelling clothes when they were dry and put them in the basket. He was also responsible, if he was outside and it started to storm, for rushing in and shouting a warning so the dry laundry could be gathered. A neighbor's burning trash also had to be reported on wash day. Smoky-smelling laundry had to be done over, cutting into play time, and thus was a curse on the land and a grave deprivation.

20

rooftops, pigeons, red light, sleepovers

A FTER SUPPER WE PLAYED night games in the summer street— mainly hide and seek, pom-pom-pullaway, red rover, annie-ay-over, gray wolf, and kick the can. Girls played with us; we did not object. Sometimes it was even interesting to stand around talking to girls. Fathers came out to water the front lawns with hoses; our mothers sat in chairs on front porches to catch the breeze or walked next door or across the street to talk to a neighbor.

Leaving the girls, we might check our pigeon traps on the roofs of uptown buildings. We knew all the fire escapes and outside stairs. Quiet, hiding in the darkness, we crept from roof to roof, sometimes sticking our heads over the edge to look down at lit Center Street and the people who didn't know we were above them.

But we never caught any pigeons. We envied the flocks of pigeons; they were always flying around doing nothing. Dean Gray and Russ Madsen had pigeons. One day Dean fed his flock from a small sack of wheat he found in the garage. All his pigeons died. It was poisoned wheat his mother had bought for rats. The stricken birds all lay in the driveway on their backs with their feet in the air. Dean wept.

Hiking in the hills above Provo one afternoon, much to my astonishment and that of my friends, I knocked down two pigeons with a flock shot. Standing in his yard, the farmer cussed and yelled at us, but in vain. We picked and cleaned the pigeons without the benefit of water and spitted them over a sagebrush fire. My two roasted shoes would have been more succulent.

Evenings sometimes we went to play football on the depot lawn or to sit and watch the freights come roaring through. A box above each railroad car wheel held batting that had to be kept oiled to lubricate the wheel. If a wheel didn't get enough oil, it caught on fire from the friction. We called these hot boxes. We counted hot boxes, the flames lighting up the whole side of the car and casting shadows as the freight sped through the night. It was possible for a wheel to burn out and fall off, causing a train wreck, but we were never fortunate enough to see this happen, although we anticipated the pleasure of such a catastrophe.

Sometimes a big Malley would stop at the depot, and we would stand next to the great wheels in the clouds of emitted steam, the whole massive, black machine alive with interior rumblings, the engineer looking down at us from the cab. Then slowly the drive wheels taller than our heads would turn, the big silver drive rods pushing back and forth, and the Malley and the long line of cars would slowly vanish into the night, leaving us standing bereft.

Going home from the depot, if one of us had salvaged a spool of thin copper wire from some electric motor, we would hold one end of the wire and throw the spool over the electrical power line that ran the Orem interurban along Fifth South. When the wire grounded, it went up in a flash of blue flame, which we enjoyed.

Or if we weren't in any hurry and it was late enough on a Saturday night, we might go by the Utahna Gardens to look through the windows and see adults dancing, their arms around each other. It seemed like a strange thing to see, maybe even sinful, especially married Sixth Ward brothers and sisters dancing with somebody else, moving slowly around the big hall laughing and talking. But we guessed it was okay because Bishop Oldroyd didn't come to preach repentance.

A house on Second South had a red porch light, and we used to hide in the weeds of a vacant lot across the street to see who went in and out and what they did. We'd heard something about what red lights outside a house meant, and we saw a lot of men going in and out, but it was very confused knowledge, and our vigil was fruitless, our curiosity never satisfied.

Sometimes we had loogie fights under the corner street lamps after it got dark. You kept sniffing and clearing your throat until you had a big loogie, and then you spit it high in the air and hoped it would come down on one of the other guys, who couldn't see it coming because of the darkness. You fought alone, running back and forth in the street trying to get off a shot. You had to keep looking up so you wouldn't get hit. I caught Dan Larsen right between the eyes one night, and he chased me for three blocks describing the different ways he was going to murder me. It was a perfect shot.

At ten o'clock we were called in to go to bed, unless we had a sleepover, fathers and mothers or older brothers and sisters shouting our names from the front porch or sidewalk until we acknowledged we were still alive, but quietly.

"I'm coming. Good grief, Mom. Can't I play for just ten more minutes?"

"You've played enough. Tomorrow's another day."

"Gee."

If we slept over, it was usually on a friend's back lawn or in a tent put up for the occasion, not in the house, where there was really little place, for we did not have bedrooms of our own. Later, the neighborhood fast asleep, the shadows dark, we dared each other to run around the block in our shorts, in the end all of us taking turns. You ran barefooted, hiding behind hedges, fences, trees, and rosebushes if a car came down the street, terrified that a cop might reach out and grab you and put you in jail.

We heard rumors of boys running around the block bare-assed, but we'd never seen that. It would have seemed like a strange thing to do unless you planned to stop somewhere to go swimming. Common decency and belief in civilized behavior required that you wore at least your shorts in the neighborhood, whatever the temptations.

And then, not knowing exactly when it happened, we fell asleep to the sound of crickets and the far-off lonesome wail of a train going through Provo to some faraway and distant place.

21

tracks, flare gas, Park Ro She, wander lust

IF WE CHOSE NOT TO SPEND our summer day at the Crusher or at the lake, we headed south down University Avenue, followed the millrace to the county fairgrounds, CCC Camp, golf course, the sewer, and the fields. The millrace flowed under the railroad tracks in a tunnel, coming out again on the other side. We waded up into the tunnel to sit on a ledge in the black darkness and smoke cedar bark, our voices echoing if we spoke too loudly in our discussions about life, the ends of our burning cedar-bark cigars our only light. We regretted that there wasn't a deep hole to swim in. Swimming in absolute darkness, not knowing where your skin ended and the water began, would have been wonderful, our bodies melting into water.

The CCC Camp, a series of barracks, held no special interest except for a pet cow elk that belonged to the camp and used to chase us. We sneaked from building to building, stopping to peek around corners. If the elk saw us, we'd scatter and hide or get through the fence. She never did catch any of us, but we had the pleasure of being terrified.

The county fair exhibition halls stood locked and empty. We looked forward to the fair in September. We liked to see all the different breeds of prize chickens and rabbits. We liked the sheep and the pigs too fat to walk and the milk cows. We even liked the fruits, vegetables, flowers, and handiwork exhibits. Crowds filled the halls, people laughing and talking. Out on the midway we stopped at the stands to buy hamburgers, hot dogs, and drinks and spend our few nickels playing the games for stuffed animals and ceramic dolls that we never won, particularly at the shooting gallery. We knew everything was rigged, but still we played, still we had faith in our own ability and the final goodness of man. We liked the carnival rides too and all the music and lights. The fair meant the end to summer and the beginning of fall and school again.

The Barnum and Bailey Circus set up at the fairgrounds every summer. We went down to help with the tents to get free tickets. Along both sides of the midway leading into the big tent were all the freak shows—the fattest man in the world, the thinnest, the bearded lady, the tattooed man, the man who swallowed swords and ate fire, and the smallest couple in the world.

We boys believed in freaks. It's a word we often used to describe each other or situations in general—freaky. For a dime, a man with no arms would write your name on a small card. The card was held by two clips, and he wrote with the pen between his big toe and the next toe. I paid my dime. The writing was the most beautiful I had ever seen. I couldn't believe it. I kept the card. I decided I would try to improve my own writing. I admired the armless man.

The circus wasn't very interesting, except for the tent. All the animals, especially the lions and tigers, seemed moth-eaten and old, the elephants' hides worn and patchy. But it was interesting to see how the elephants helped pull up the big top. We couldn't believe how big the tent was. We talked about what it would be like if it caught on fire. We'd heard of circuses burning down, all the people screaming and running out the entrance, the flames crawling up the canvas sides. All animals would get loose—the lions and tigers, free for the first time in their whole lives, attacking people, the stampeding elephants trampling everybody flat. We believed that every circus needed a King Kong who could escape.

The millrace ran through the golf course, and we followed it, searching for lost balls to sell, if the ball wasn't waterlogged and worthless. Golfers warned us we might get hit by a driven ball, but we paid little attention; however, one day a boy squatting by the side of the bank to retrieve a ball was hit in the back. He fell forward into the water but wasn't hurt, although we knew that if the ball had hit him in the head, it might have caused some damage. Yet, as we had so often been told, we knew we had thick skulls, which were some protection.

Pressing south we eventually came to the Provo sewer flowing out of a big concrete pipe into the millrace, giving enough volume for the stream to flow until it was met by the creosote ditch and Spring Creek, both increasing its depth and width, and then it flowed, somewhat diluted and purified, into the lake. We stood to watch the sewer come out of the pipe. It was instructive. An open sewer helps convince a boy that people are human, or at least that they all have bowels and bladders. There was no particular stench, nothing alarming to see, certainly no dead babies or murdered corpses, simply the gray-brown stream, which we followed down through the fields.

Usually we carried our BB guns. We shot at the carp we spooked along the shallow edges or at blackbirds. Sometimes ducks jumped off the sewer. We followed them with our guns, but we didn't shoot. The season didn't open until October. We jumped pheasants too but never shot at them. Dave Nelson had a Civil War cap and ball pistol for which he molded his own lead balls. A bridge spanned the sewer right where it came out of the pipe, and Dave and I spent one whole afternoon there shooting bottles, or trying to. It was not a very accurate weapon. There seemed to be a lot of bottles floating by or on the bank, which we tossed in.

Later when Dave had a car, a '32 Chevy we called the can car that his father had resurrected at King's Auto Salvage, we'd drive down remote mountain roads shooting at signs. None of the car doors worked, and they had to be wired shut. To shoot signs, you stood on the running board, your left arm through the open windows and around the doorpost, and you fired at the fleeting targets.

Moving farther down into the fields toward the sloughs, we played a form of killer tag in the tall clumps of bull rushes. We broke off the bull-rush seedpods to use as hand grenades, and then one side would hide and the other side would try to find the hidden foe. Letting the enemy pass, we would rise up and throw a seedpod at close range. A hit meant you were dead. In the early fall, the seedpods would explode on contact, and you tried for a head shot.

If we didn't follow the millrace and the sewer, we walked along the railroad tracks. We had no particular purpose in mind, just followed the tracks in the fierce shimmering summer heat. We pulled from ties the burned-out ends of spiked fusees to throw at the telli-wackers along the tracks. The boy who stuck up the most fusees won. We picked up railroad spikes to look at, but they were too heavy to carry in our pockets, so we dropped them. We had contests to see who could walk the farthest on the track without falling off.

We liked to watch the big freights and passenger

trains coming roaring through. Hobos waved to us from the open freight cars. Soldiers in the troop trains waved. We liked trains. We knew they went to distant places, and if we kept walking we would arrive at these places, but we didn't intend to do that. We were satisfied to live in Provo. As boys we didn't seem to have any particular wanderlust, other than to fight in the war or go to Yellowstone Park.

Passing the Ironton pig-iron plant, we saw the high column of flame when they were burning flare gas. The air always smelled sulfury around Ironton. We'd stop to watch the huge ladles of molten slag emptied on the dump, the slag like lava. We'd heard that a hobo had lain down on the warm slag to sleep one winter night and they'd poured a whole ladle on him. You were supposed to be able to see the form of his body under the slag if you knew where to look, but we couldn't ever find it. High school boys drove their girlfriends out at night to park and watch the slag being dumped. Dave Nelson's dad worked at Ironton.

If we found deep-enough water in the fields, we went swimming. The only place to do that was Spring Creek where it poured into a big hole. One afternoon when we were following the tracks past the pipe plant, the guard at the gate stopped us.

"I hope you kids aren't swimming in the creek down there. It's the Springville sewer. You know that, right?"

"Oh, sure. Thanks."

"Well, you don't want to be swimming in any sewer."

"Nope."

We were appreciative of his concern. We knew enough of the world to understand that some adults would not have warned us of our danger. But we knew it wasn't a sewer. We knew what a sewer looked like. We were smarter than that.

We typically stopped to pee in unison on any of the one-strand electric cattle fences we came across in the fields. Pee being a good conductor, the resulting tingling coming up into the vitals wasn't an unpleasant sensation, depending on the low voltage, of course. Voltages differed.

If we had the money, sometimes we continued on over to Park Ro She, a Springville swimming pool. Park Ro She had two long pools divided by a cement wall. On a long rope hanging down from the ceiling, you could swing out and drop into the south pool. The swing was a main attraction.

One day walking along the tracks, we scared up a hen pheasant that flew over some gondola cars that a railroad man was sweeping out. As the pheasant flew over him, the man raised his broom and knocked it down. Later, coming back we walked by the cars and talked to the man. It was Max Hodson, Owen's brother. He showed us the pheasant in his lunch bucket. We thought that was really great. Two or three years later, we met Max under the old wooden Geneva Bridge across the lower Provo River. He was fishing, on leave from the army. It was the last time we saw him, for he was later killed in action.

22

45–70, grizzly bears, escaped maniac, ledges of gold

WE DIDN'T CARRY OUR .22s down to the fields. We knew that a bullet could travel for a mile and might kill somebody. It was an unwritten rule. We didn't question it, although we would have liked our .22s to shoot magpies, very smart birds you couldn't get close to. A .22 was a mountain gun. Our entrance to the mountains was Slate Canyon, a wide deep canyon between Maple Flat and Buckley Mountains. A hike took all day. Nobody encouraged us to go. A hike was hot and exhausting in the summer heat. We might hike five or six miles, maybe ten if we climbed Provo Peak, over eleven thousand feet high.

You had to sort of plan a hike. You needed a lunch and a canteen and your .22 and at least a box of shells. Or you might carry a shotgun. Dave and I both had 45–70 Springfield rifles we'd bought through the Herter's Catalog, brand new, still in the Cosmoline, wonderful twelve-pound Spanish American War rifles with a big hammer, a trap-door chamber, that took a three-inch black-powder cartridge and fired a 405-grain lead slug. Dave also had a double-barreled ten-gauge muzzle-loading shotgun he sometimes took.

No parent ever offered to give us a ride to the mouth of the canyon. Carrying our guns and our lunches, we walked up Third South to Seventh East and then south to the road that took us to the mouth of Slate. A trail built by the CCC led high up on the south side of the canyon. It was not uncommon to see groups of boys carrying guns walking down a Provo street headed for the mountains or fields.

In the dusty trail we looked for bobcat, coyote, and deer tracks, which we sometimes found. What we wanted to see were bear and cougar tracks, but we never did, although there were bear and cougar in the hills. We regretted the death of all the grizzly bears, ferocious and almost impossible to kill and able to kill you. And we would have liked to see a band of wild, untamed Indians who would befriend us, make us blood brothers, and take us into the tribe so we would never have to go home again. We didn't think we would be missed particularly.

Climbing higher, always watching for rattlesnakes because they could bring horrible, swollen death, we stopped to look down the canyon toward Provo, the fields, and Utah Lake. Part of the pleasure of hiking was being high above the valley and being able to look down. It was a new dimension for us, the sense of being remote from an earlier life. We became explorers, mountain men, and Indians. We particularly longed to be Indians, to wear only loincloths, to throw off civilized restraint, spend our whole lives hunting and making war and maybe even making love, which we'd begun to understand was not an unpleasant activity. We wanted to wear magnificent headdresses, paint our bodies, wear our hair down to our ankles, and dance the war dance around a big fire all night to beating drums.

The State Mental Hospital stood near the mouth of Slate Canyon, and patients escaped, sometimes a body being found up Slate Canyon. The one thing we truly feared was an escaped maniac who would leap out at

us with a long knife and murder us all before we could
shoot, our blood-covered bodies to be found later with
our throats slashed, the look of approaching horror and
death still in our eyes. But this never happened, however often we imagined it.

We shot at everything—rocks, stumps, squirrels,
rock chucks, flying and perched birds, pinecones, lizards, rattlesnakes, flowers. If it was something alive and
moving, we argued about who got the first shot, took
turns on good targets.

We shot for the pleasure of it, aiming, hearing the
report, feeling the kick, the pleasure of holding a gun,
the cool metal, the polished wood. We liked to hold the
shells, feed them into the tube magazine or the clip. I
longed to own a Browning automatic, really a semiau-
tomatic, the best .22, but I could never afford one. You
could just keep pulling the trigger and shooting until the
magazine, holding many shells, was empty.

A box of .22 ammunition held fifty shells, either shorts,
long rifle, or hollow point. We liked hollow points best
because they were supposed to explode on contact, were
more deadly. Sometimes we had to chip in to buy a box
of shells, every boy getting his fair share. It was pleasing
to have a whole box of shells yourself, empty it into your
Levi's pocket, feel the weight, know you had that many
shots left

When we killed a rodent or bird, we always stood
to examine it, see where the slug went in, see the blood,
look at the eyes. And we talked about the shot, estimat-
ed the yardage, because the farther away the better shot
you were. Dave Nelson was the best shot. I wasn't very
good. You were ranked according to how good a shot
you were.

We had no regrets, didn't think about having killed
something wild and free that had been alive, didn't

consider its right to live, that it had a spirit like we'd been taught in church. We didn't make the connection. We were never warned about killing, told only to be careful and not shoot each other. A boy had a right to a gun or guns, was expected to enjoy shooting. If his father hunted, he would go with him to shoot deer, ducks, and pheasants in the fall to bring home food. Or he would go with friends or alone. A deer was an important source of meat. Being a good shot was vital.

We wanted to kill a grouse or a cottontail so we could cook it over a fire on a spit and, crouching around the fire, break off the pieces of meat with our fingers and eat like Indians and mountain men did. But we never did this, had to be satisfied with our peanut butter and jelly sandwiches.

We filled our canteens from springs and from what we called water mines, two concrete boxes fed by the State Hospital water line, which came down Slate. Where the metal pipe hung suspended from a cable to cross the canyon, it was full of bullet holes, the water spurting out, but we didn't shoot at it with our .22s. They weren't powerful enough to penetrate the metal. You had to have a deer rifle for that. We also didn't shoot off the insulators on the power lines at the mouth of the canyon. You had to have a deer rifle for that too, and you could be arrested if they caught you, and you might start a fire and burn down the whole mountain.

We looked for gold. We believed in finding gold, ledges of gold. We knew miners had looked for gold in Slate Canyon. We'd been inside the old prospects, tunnels going back a hundred or two hundred feet before they stopped, some in solid rock. So we knew there was gold. We stopped to pick up shining rocks or those that showed any kind of mineralization. Standing in a circle, we examined what we found. In our pockets we carried home pieces to show Mr. Sorensen, our science teacher at the Dixon, to ask him if it was gold. Sometimes we carried our mother's pie tins with us to pan for gold when the water came down Slate in the spring.

Or we expected to find buried Spanish gold, Montezuma's treasure in a great long secret cave, or locked, iron strong boxes from the robbed stagecoach or mail train; we fully expected to see the corner of the strong box sticking up out of the ground where it had been buried. And although we never found this wealth, we were not discouraged. We stopped to pick up old rifle shell casings, some green with age. We argued about whether it was from some deer hunter, Indian fight, or some miner protecting his claim. It really didn't matter which. Our imaginations covered all the possibilities.

We kept our eyes peeled for dynamite. We knew that prospectors and miners sometimes left dynamite in old mine shafts. We'd heard of boys lucky enough to find dynamite, a whole case, and fuses, and caps, spending the day blowing up things—standing trees, logs, boulders, ledges, tunnels, caves, and old shacks and cabins. But we were never so fortunate. We made carbide bombs. We also mixed our own black powder from sulfur, saltpeter, and carbon, but it wasn't very reliable bomb material.

Robert Harris made a whole packsack full of bombs that had about three times the power of a cherry bomb or a silver salute, firecrackers that could blow off three or four fingers at a time, and he and I spent the whole day hiking up Rock Canyon and out Slate blowing up protruding rocks, flowing springs, badger holes, logs, dead standing trees, and other things as opportunity presented itself.

Cordon Cullimore had an uncle named Cory Hanks who was blinded and had both hands blown off when he picked up a box of dynamite caps. He was eighteen and working on a prospect above Heber Valley with a friend. The dynamite caps had been sitting in the sun all day, and when he picked up the box, they exploded. His friend tied his wrists with rawhide thongs so Hanks wouldn't bleed to death and went for help. Hanks tried to untie the knots with his teeth but couldn't do it. A cheerful old man, he'd spent his life as a lecturer and teacher. I was very impressed by Mr. Hanks when I met him at Cordon's. To eat he had a spoon shaped like a bracelet that fit over his right wrist. I was surprised that dynamite caps were that powerful.

Climbing higher in the hot sun, we left the CCC trails, climbed up through ledges and cliffs, groves of quaking aspen, up ridges, to the tops of mountains, to Provo Peak, Camel's Pass, the Big Pine Grove, and Middle Mountain. Standing on a ridge or peak, we believed we stood where no white man had ever stood before, felt free and separate from everybody else, took off our shirts to feel more. We regretted only that we didn't have places to swim, clear, deep pools filled by hidden springs, our bodies yearning for that.

From the top of Provo Peak, if the day was clear, we saw ridge after ridge, mountain after mountain, all in different shades of bluish purple, falling away against the horizon, saw maybe fifty or sixty miles in all directions, this the extent of our known world. Silent, we stood watching, awed a little finally at how big things were, how far the world stretched away into vastness, something we had not before understood.

23

snow, Monopoly, stove, Christmas, parrot

WINTERS WE DIDN'T ROAM so much, our summer world become cold, and of course we had to go to school. In our house we had only the kitchen stove, but if you had a front room you had a potbellied stove. I liked my friends' potbellied stoves. Lying or sitting on the floor playing Monopoly, Chinese checkers, ordinary checkers, and Rook, you always knew how close you had to get to stay warm. It was important to be just warm enough.

Your friend's mom or dad always knew when to put on another lump or two of coal, when to poke the fire, the orange flame visible through the isinglass door panels, when to open or close the damper or shake the grate. A fire had to be cared for, encouraged, all the adjustments just right. All the family was drawn to the fire on winter evenings. If you were lucky, your friend's mom gave you hot chocolate and cookies, or maybe you made popcorn. You always took off your galoshes before you went into the house.

We counted time by Halloween, Thanksgiving, Christmas, New Year's, Valentine's, Fourth of July, the start and end of school, and the hunting seasons when we were old enough to shoot. The duck season opened first and lasted until January. We prayed for storms then, driving snow storms to bring the ducks in off the lake. It was never too cold, the snow never too deep, the wind never too fierce to go hunting. You heard the whistling wings first if snow fell gently without noise, the big migrating northern mallards dropping down, appearing suddenly above us out of the whiteness.

Clad in hip boots, gloves, heavy coats and hats, scarves, shell vests, carrying our shotguns across the handlebars or in one hand, guiding the bike with the other, we rode happily into the storm. Weary, face wooden with cold, hands and feet numb, two or three fallen ducks in our game pockets, we returned. Dave's mother fed us hot chocolate and heavy chocolate cake with blue frosting, which helped get me the five or six blocks to home, where my mother told me when I coughed that I probably had pneumonia and would I ever get any sense, which she doubted. She gave me the red hot-water bottle, which I wrapped in a towel and clutched under the covers to my increasingly precious body, moved close to Bob and Rowland for warmth. In the winter we brothers argued about who got to sleep in the warm middle.

The summer-porch windows were thick with frost. Outside, the mountains gleamed in their whiteness. The first skiff of snow had come to the top of Mount Timp, the valley's highest, in mid-September, then melted away with warm Indian-summer days. Timp might get a light snow by the end of deer season in October and certainly by mid-November, the snow line dropping lower and lower with each storm, until all the surrounding smaller mountains stood gleaming white against the dark night sky. When the fading light was right, Timpanogos and the east mountains turned various shades of pink and at other times blue, people on the streets stopping to turn and look, or being called out of their houses to come and look at Timp before the evening glory vanished.

Except for hunting, bizzing, snowball fights, building

igloos, and occasionally going down to the fields to ice skate, we weren't outside much. The closest hill for sledding was Temple Hill, too far away for the thrill afforded. Bizzing was the most popular sport, but you had to have just the right condition, freezing cold and icy-slick roads. To biz you waited for a slow passing car or one just pulling out onto the road and then ran out, grabbed the rear bumper, and squatted down, your leather-soled shoes gliding over the ice.

With three or four boys hanging on, you could, if you were skilled, get the car weaving back and forth down the road. But the driver inevitably slowed down, opened his window, and told you to get the hell off, or stopped the car and chased you away, shouting and waving his arms, which was at least half the fun.

Another sport involving cars was to hide behind a hedge or fence and pelt an oncoming car with snowballs. This too took skill. You had to calculate speed, elevation, and trajectory, and you all had to throw at once so that the attack was coordinated, five or six missiles striking at once. You hoped to hit the windshield or windows, but a good solid hit against the roof or even the sides gave a satisfactory thunk that could stop a car and bring out a driver yelling for your blood.

It was an error, of course, to bombard a carful of high-school seniors who chased you down, washed your face with snow, stuffed snow down your shirt, and snowballed you out of sight, or perhaps pantsed you and threw your Levi's into a tree. Climbing a winter tree barelegged afforded little real pleasure.

We boys looked forward to the big Sixth Ward Christmas party and program and all the treats you could eat. One year during the war, Darwin Luke, dressed like a soldier, sat at a desk sadly writing a letter, and I sang "White Christmas" — "I'll be home for Christmas, just you wait and see" —for once bringing it off without singing flat. I wanted to be the soldier, writing a last letter just before going into battle.

Neighbors had trees in the front windows but didn't string many lights outside. Provo City decorated Center Street, and all the stores had Christmas windows and store decorations. Everybody always came uptown for the Christmas parade.

The big Santa Claus sled with six or eight reindeer on a long flatbed truck was the main event, Santa throwing candy to the kids. Somehow Santa's reindeer looked strangely familiar, and then one Christmas I understood that they came from the high shelves at Hank Smith's pool hall. Although I could never prove this, standing in the doorway on summer days looking up, I was confident that the mule-deer bucks were metamorphosed into Santa's reindeer. It was a pleasing prospect, all those smoky bucks pulling Santa's sled.

My mother always borrowed three hundred dollars for Christmas because, as she said, the kids deserved a good Christmas. Every month I carried the twenty-five dollars up to Personal Finance to make the payment; they knew me by name. Mom didn't like to wrap presents. When I was nine and gone to bed on Christmas Eve, she woke me to come and wrap the presents. One winter night I was walking up Center Street when a man stopped me and asked what I was doing uptown and didn't I know it was Christmas Eve. I didn't. Christmas was important; Christmas Eve not.

Dressed like Santa Claus, Uncle Harry Heal always came to our house to hand us kids sacks of candy. Neighbors and relatives, who thought us poor, brought us sacks of flour, sugar, and potatoes to help see us through the winter. The women my mother cleaned houses for brought her gifts.

Our mother made us wait for our father to come before we could open our presents. We kept running out to the front sidewalk to see if he was coming. He always brought a brown wicker basket filled with oranges, his arm through the handle as he walked. Like my friends, we had a big Christmas turkey dinner. Mother made carrot pudding with her special sauce. Christmas afternoon Dave Nelson and I always went down in the fields to shoot crows. For Christmas one of my gifts was a box of shotgun shells.

After Christmas the long winter was dreary for me and my friends. We longed for spring and the end of school. For Valentine's we made a big red cardboard heart, tied a string to it, put it on some girl's porch, rang or knocked, and hollered "Valentine's." When she reached down to pick it up, we jerked it away and ran laughing down the street, dragging the red heart behind us. We were not kind.

There were no weather forecasts. We waited for the piled-high snow to melt, to see the water running in rivulets down the streets and into the gutters, a sure sign of spring. We waited for the robins to come back and watched, after the valley floor was free of snow, the snow line slowly creep up the sides of the mountains. But always there was a heavy storm or two in late March or early April to turn our world white again and fill us with despair, and after that the heavy spring rains. We longed for the hot shirtless days and our remembered long summers of freedom, which, now that we were older and working, were less to be anticipated than before.

24

Mr. Buttle, showers, dances, jokes, sex education

LEAVING THE FRANKLIN and going to the Dixon, the things we boys looked forward to most were six different classes a day from six different teachers, our own hall lockers, gym, weekly dances, and dating. Possible classes were math, science, English, gym, history, shop, typing, and boys' chorus. Nothing fancy. Perhaps the most anticipated change was gym, for which you had to wear gym trunks, an athletic supporter, gym shoes, and you got to play basketball in a gymnasium and shower afterward, which we appreciated deeply. Most of us had tubs at home, not showers.

Being able to shower was important, seemed more luxurious, male, and athletic. Not having your mother or sister yelling through the bathroom door was nice too. With the multiple showerheads spouting hot water, the steam rising in clouds, there were towel fights, general rioting, and concern about who was the manliest, although we weren't sure why this was as important as it seemed to be.

At thirteen and fourteen, we were on our own regarding sex. There was no sex education, and parents typically told boys nothing about sex, other than perhaps to put a state-published sex-education pamphlet on his pillow, with no introductory or later comment. In church we were told to be clean and pure, to practice self-restraint, to not pollute our bodies, without further explanation, except possibly for a local doctor who was dragged in to talk to the Aaronic Priesthood youth about sex in the vaguest terms possible.

Thus, we were free to acquire our own vocabularies from each other and older boys, hear and repeat stories and jokes, and endure our own experiences and new dreams. Slowly we moved into the world of our own sexuality—the wonder, anticipation, exaggeration, disappointment—just as generations of pubescent Dixon Junior High boys had before us, and with the same measure of guilt, mystery, and pleasure.

Schoolyard fights dropped off, perhaps because we were more closely supervised, a teacher having us always under eye, but perhaps too because we were bigger now and could do more damage, and the girls didn't seem quite so entertained. Still, you had to fight if challenged. Cowardice was not acceptable. For some other boy to threaten to pin your ears back was a serious challenge.

It was interesting having a different teacher for every class—Mr. Gould for math; Mr. Knudsen, gym; Mr. Sorensen, science; Mr. Buttle, English, our homeroom class. In the ninth grade Mr. Buttle's sixth-period class was all boys. Mr. Buttle told us that if we were good during the week, every Friday we could tell jokes and he would read to us, to which we happily agreed. The first Friday the first joke told by the son of a BYU professor shocked even Mr. Buttle, and that ended the joke telling, but Mr. Buttle still read us stories.

Although I tried hard to be a perfect student and was advancing steadily toward my Eagle badge, I had the misfortune one day to annoy the choir teacher, who, grabbing me by the collar, opened the double door with my head, a sobering experience. Another time, sitting behind Jim Rhodes, I made a noise and roused Mr. Buttle's ire. Thinking Jim guilty, Mr. Buttle cuffed him. I wanted to stand and accept the blame, but I lacked the required courage, which made me feel less of myself as an Eagle-seeking Scout. Jim never blamed me. Perhaps he had a guilty conscience resulting from previous unpunished infractions or had made a simultaneous noise. I never asked.

Mr. Buttle chewed tobacco and would raise the hinged window to spit it outside. Legend had it that once some boys polished the window, and Mr. Buttle—or Buttle, as we called him—thinking the window open, spit all over it. We enjoyed the story, true or not. Mr. Buttle worked Saturdays and summers in Bob's Billiards on University Avenue, and when we walked by, we boys would push open the swinging door and call a greeting. Mr. Buttle took the big cigar out of his mouth, said hello, and asked us what the hell we thought we were doing. We liked Mr. Buttle.

We had Friday dances. You could hold a girl as close as you wanted and dance slowly. The music didn't matter. Having both of your arms around a girl, her head on your shoulder, feeling her hair against the side of your face, smelling her perfume was wonderful. I used to twirl a lot with a girl named Colleen Collins, who lost hold of me one afternoon, and I crashed into a wall. Colleen was strong.

Girls were okay; they had become necessary, for some reason. We started to date but cautiously, usually going in groups of eight or ten to avoid prevalent dangers. We had to walk wherever we went. Practicing great restraint, we boys didn't reach out to hold hands but kept our hands in our pockets or pinioned under our arms.

One day a rumor spread like wildfire among the Dixon boys that a girl, broad-shouldered with a high and heavy chest, wearing a tight, deep-cut V-necked sweater, had come bouncing joyfully down the stairs, lost momentary control, and a revelation had ensued. We longed ardently for this marvelous event to have been true, wished wholeheartedly we'd been there, but could find not one boy who might offer eye-witness evidence, so we had to rely only on our imaginations to satisfy our yearning.

Our summers and after-school hours were not entirely free now; we had to have serious money for guns, ammunition, fishing equipment, shows, bicycles, to pay for our own clothes, and even for girls. You were expected to start helping pay your own way, the war making part-time summer jobs easier to get.

Your first major financial obligation was to buy your own clothes, finally giving your mother something to brag about in conversation with neighborhood mothers whose sons weren't quite so industrious and might be expected to run naked if they didn't hurry up and rustle a job. Rustling a job was very important. We knew about rustling cattle but weren't quite sure how to get out and rustle a job, as we were admonished to do. You were also told, now that you had a few dollars, not to spend it like a drunken sailor or let it burn a hole in your pocket.

We worked a few hours a day or on alternate days or perhaps only Saturdays, sweeping out offices, washing dishes in restaurants, doing yard work, picking fruits and vegetables, and bagging groceries. One of the best places to work summers was Pleasant Grove Cannery down by the viaduct on West Center Street, but you had to be sixteen.

My first good-paying job was catching night crawlers, the large nocturnal worm admired by fishermen as bait. I sold them wholesale to Mrs. Kirkwood, a woman my father knew who lived next to the fire station. I usually caught three or four quarts a night, going from

lawn to lawn and garden to garden with my flashlight
and gallon can, holding the flashlight in my mouth when
the worms were thick so I could use both hands. At fifty
cents a quart I usually earned two dollars a night, which
was big money. Mrs. Kirkwood always paid me in silver,
the wonderful large, heavy silver dollars and the lesser
fifty-cent pieces and quarters, but still silver, my pocket
heavy with silver every night.

I left the house as soon as it got dark, usually about
nine, and worked till two or three in the morning. In the
three years I caught crawlers, no one ever hollered at me
or chased me off. Men and boys were often out catching
crawlers to go fishing with, so having someone moving
across your lawn with a flashlight wasn't unusual. The
only time I was ever scared was up on the State Hospital
lawns. I kept thinking some crazy person was going to
leap out of the bushes and kill me or carry me away, although I wasn't sure where or why. I kept looking around
and shining my flashlight on the bushes and trees, until
I got so scared that I jumped on my bike and rode away.
One night going home I was so tired I fell asleep on my
bike and crashed, but I didn't break anything.

When I was in the eighth grade, and a few months
before my father died, we moved to Logan, a small town
a hundred and twenty miles north of Provo. We lived
there a year.

My first Logan job was delivering the *Tribune* on
freezing winter mornings on my hilly route up by the
university. A baying bloodhound chased me, my glasses
froze to my watery eyes, I often spilled on the icy roads,
and the customers were loath to pay the one dollar a
month. One Sunday morning I spilled, the heavy papers
sliding down the hill. Filled with a final despair, I sat
in the middle of the road hoping to freeze to death as
quickly as possible.

After I quit my route, I got a job washing dishes at the Dairy Lunch. It was my first job working with adults and the beginning of my entry into the adult world. A boy had to enter the adult world sooner or later, and working with adults was a typical and useful way. And the adults, whether they intended to or not, took up his education, for better or for worse.

My mother didn't have the faintest notion that I was being educated on the job, and neither did I. A boy was just expected to grow up, one way or the other. I took meals to the prisoners in the city jail, becoming acquainted with the inevitable consequences of theft, assault, burglary, drunkenness, and debauchery in general. A waitress with long dark hair taught me how to kiss, and a young fry cook gave me somewhat detailed instructions on how not to get a girl pregnant, intimating to me the burden of my fertility, or perhaps approaching fertility, and the possible terrible consequences.

As soon as school was over, I jumped on my bike and raced down to work. All the dishes, glasses, and silverware from lunch awaited me in a big, square, high-sided galvanized bin, and these had to be washed, dried, and ready for the supper trade. I had two deep sinks and a drain board. The owner, who was also the cook, made the soap. He raised pigs in a barn outside of town, slopping them with the wet garbage from the kitchen. He slaughtered and cut up the pigs himself, and he served a lot of uninspected pork. He made his own soap from the fat, boiling it in washtubs on the stove. This was the dish soap I used after it had been cut up into chunks.

His wife, who worked in the front, pretty well had control of things. Her husband liked to slip out the back, go two or three doors down to a saloon to get a beer, and play a quiet game of pool. She was always coming into the kitchen and asking me where he was and then sending me after him. He would cuss, ask me why a man couldn't have a beer in peace, a reasonable question that I couldn't answer, and then follow me back to the restaurant. His wife never said anything to him. She knew where he'd been and why. Once he was back in the kitchen, she was satisfied.

They were the only married couple I'd ever really been around on a daily basis, other than my parents before the divorce. This marriage didn't seem strange or conflicted; they got along pretty well. They'd learned to accommodate each other. I added this observation to the store of knowledge I was accumulating about adults.

In the spring, we moved back to Provo. The café owner and his wife said I could live with them free of charge if I would stay and work the summer, because good dishwashers were hard to get. But I was homesick for Provo and my hooligan friends.

In Logan I had the only teacher I truly hated. Delivering the *Tribune* on winter mornings, I was often late for school because the truck from Salt Lake couldn't get through snowy Sardine Pass. The teacher always stopped class to make special note of my lateness and get the class laughing at me. I'd never been humiliated like that before in my whole life. I left school two weeks early to return to Provo, and on the last day I went up to the teacher's office to tell the old wretch—one of my mother's terms for miscreants—to go to hell both in general and in particular. He wasn't there, a huge disappointment, but I walked away admiring my own resolve.

25

gadwalls, best shot, storms, whistling wings, kayak

AT FOURTEEN WE COULD HUNT ducks and pheasants legally
but still had to wait two more years to hunt deer. Filled
with anticipation and desire, almost pure joy, terribly
impatient, we waited for the seasons to open, duck and
deer in October and the pheasants in November. Bird
hunting was better during the war because there weren't
so many hunters. But the deer hunting wasn't so good
because there weren't enough hunters to drive the deer
and keep them moving.

On September afternoons after school, Dave Nelson
and I each got half a gunnysack of his dad's duck decoys
and rode our bikes down to the fields to some springs
we knew. We set out the decoys and lay on the gunnysacks to watch incoming ducks. We needed the thrill of
seeing ducks.

In the early evening ducks came in off Utah Lake in
singles, pairs, and small flocks, the big northern flights
not down yet. The sun setting, we watched the silhouetted ducks coming in, heard their whistling wings,
their calls, and, kneeling, we raised our arms to pre-
tend we were shooting. We breathed in deep the sharp
fall smell of the fields and the springs. We liked the big
greenheads best; they were the best duck. Walking back
to our bikes through the fields, we heard their wings,

stopped to see them shadowed against the faintly lit sky.

Dave's father was the best duck hunter I'd ever known. He made his own hollow wooden duck decoys, built his own sneak boat, and raised Labrador retrievers. He was the best shot I'd ever seen. Dave was good, but he wasn't as good as his father. You had to plug your shotgun so you had only three shots, but when a flock came in, Mr. Nelson could knock down three, or if a single came over at sixty yards, he knocked it down every time. With his double-barreled Ithaca ten-gauge, with heavy loads, he knocked down ducks at eighty and ninety yards. He called ducks without using a wooden duck call, just his lips. He knew how to set out the decoys to attract the ducks, and he knew the best places to go.

Nothing was more thrilling for me at fourteen than to sit in a blind at first light watching a flock of fifteen or twenty mallards circle, starting to set their wings, and then drop, slipping the air, and Dave's father whispering to me and Dave to wait, wait, and then saying, "Now." And we stood up and started shooting, seeing the big mallards go ragged in the air, fall, and hit the water hard if they were dead, wings folded.

But I wasn't a very good shot. The limit was fifteen, and Dave and his dad always had to help shoot my birds.

We shot mallards, pintails, gadwalls, teal, spoonbills, and widgeons. We shot local ducks early in the season, waited for the big northern flocks to come down from the frozen north, sometimes thousands of ducks in the great high migrating flocks. We hoped for winds and storms to drive the ducks off Utah Lake and up into the ponds and sloughs. We hoped for geese too, the big Canada honkers, their wild cries always distant and growing fainter, never louder, the big birds vanishing, not coming toward us.

Later, sitting in your blinds eating a sandwich, you looked around and saw the mountains, Ironton, the pipe plant, the high buildings in Provo, the BYU, the sun reflecting off the windows, and to the west the shining lake. And if it were toward evening you watched the lights coming on and knew it was time to pick up the decoys and go home.

But boys didn't always hunt with their fathers. We carried our decoys and guns, wore our hip boots, rode our bikes down to the sloughs and ponds. We always looked for secret places where nobody else hunted, watched for ducks dropping in to feed. We didn't tell other boys about these ponds and springs.

Rob Harris built a two-seater wood-framed kayak from a *Boy's Life* plan, covered it with canvas, and painted the canvas three times for waterproofing. Wearing our hip boots, heavy hunting coats, vests filled with shells and another box of shells in a pocket, our guns and sacks of decoys pushed under the front and back, we paddled down the Provo sewer to Mud Lake to hunt. Sometimes the boy in back paddled, and the one in front shot hawks, owls, snipes, and herons that we jumped or that flew across the sewer in front of us. Any flying bird was fair game.

We had no sense of doing anything wrong, our pleasure too great to allow for reflection. We didn't think about the resurrected ducks flying around heaven and if they would know who shot them and what they would do other than just fly around. All the animals and birds in the Garden of Eden were tame, not wild, the lamb and the lion liking each other, so that couldn't have been any fun either if you were a hunter. It had begun to be obvious that being religious had its drawbacks.

Thinking it was a snow goose, I once shot a whistler swan. As I walked up through the fields carrying the swan over my shoulder, its mate kept circling and crying. I tried to shoot it too, but it never came close enough.

Had the kayak capsized, Rob and I probably wouldn't have drowned, although, weighted as we were, we certainly would have sunk down into the four or five feet of water and foot or two of accumulated sewage ooze. But we didn't worry about it; we never capsized.

When Mud Lake and the sloughs froze later in the season, we walked out on the ice, set out our decoys, and covered ourselves with old white sheets we'd pilfered from our mothers' closets.

The pheasant season started after the opening of the duck and deer seasons. All summer in our trips down to the fields we'd watched for pheasants, especially after the hay and grain were cut and you could see the flocks along the edges of the fields in the early evening, maybe twelve or fifteen hens and three or four roosters. If the setting sun was just right and the rooster turned, his whole breast shone like fire. Riding our bikes down the lanes, we heard the rooster cackling, the sound sharp, sudden, and thrilling.

The best places to hunt were down along the lake and the airport, the fields below Provo, Mud Lake if it had dried up, and the fields below Springville, Spanish Fork, and around Benjamin. There were a lot of birds. In the summer evenings Dave's father drove Dave and me down just to look for birds.

The pheasant limit was three roosters, hens illegal. The season opened at eight o'clock, but you had to be out earlier if you wanted to get a good field. You had to be all lined up or out of the cars standing in a group, or somebody else would take your field. Few hunters had dogs. You had to drive the pheasants. The best thing to do was to drive a cornfield, with a line of hunters moving through and others lined up at the bottom of the field to block the birds and make them jump. But you had to be careful not to shoot somebody.

In the first hour it sounded like a war—bam, bam, bam, bam, bam, bam, three or four hunters shooting at the same bird, or perhaps a whole line of hunters if the bird flew down the line, men shouting, "Rooster! Rooster!" or, with less enthusiasm, "Hen," or "My bird! My bird!" And you'd see a hunter run out from the line to pick up a downed pheasant.

Staying in line, walking along, you waited for a bird to jump, brought up your shotgun, lowered it if it was a hen, disappointed, shouting "Hen." A big rooster coming out at your feet cackling, brilliant in the sun, was terrifying and wonderful, sent a thrill all the way through you. You snapped your shotgun to your shoulder, pulled down on him, swung with him, fired, wanted to see him fold in a puff of feathers, see him fall, run and pick him up, hold him warm in your hands, see how beautiful he was, hold him up for the others to see, hear them say "Good shot, good shot," and then put him in your game pocket with his long tail sticking out, feeling that weight.

But I often missed, and Dave or his dad or somebody else knocked the bird down.

"What's the matter—can't you hit 'em, Doug? You got to shoot better than that."

I couldn't hit a bird flying into me or across in front of me, but if I jumped a bird, I could sometimes knock it down. One day shooting my single-shot twelve-gauge, I shot a whole box of shells, twenty-five shells in a box, one shot per bird, and never killed a bird. Very disappointing.

The pheasant season lasted three days, the duck season until the end of December, and after that we hunted crows. There was no season and no limit. But nobody ate crows; we killed them just for fun. At night they roosted in a grove of dead cottonwoods down below Kuhni's by-products plant.

In the evenings, coming in high, thousands of them, the flock trailed off across the fields for miles. And when they spiraled down to the cottonwoods, the noise was a great whirring of wings mixed with the cawing. Catching the black crows against the glowing horizon, you could shoot until it was dark. You could shoot magpies the same way. They were smart; you couldn't get within shotgun range, but in the evening when they came into the high willow hedges to roost, they were easy to kill.

When the crows migrated in the early spring, we stopped hunting birds. We started hunting jackrabbits again.

26

Diamond Fork, M-1, four-point, gang hunt, red

DURING THE WAR WE TALKED about buying an M-1 to hunt deer or maybe a carbine when the war was over. But the M-1 would be best, clip-loaded and eight shots like a machine gun. And we wanted walkie-talkies so we could talk to each other across the ridges, advise each other of bucks moving up the draw and organize the drives. But mostly we wanted a four-wheel drive Jeep to drive back into the hills on the roads no truck could travel. We saw Jeeps in the war movies and weekly war newsreels pulling through deep mud and up narrow, rocky mountain roads, so we knew they would be wonderful for hunting. Boys wanted bazookas, hand grenades, and machine guns too, but just for blowing up things, not for hunting.

The deer season started the third Saturday in October. Friday, and even Thursday, cars, pickups, and trucks moved along Highway 89 on Third South headed for the deer camps. Long before we could hunt or even be in the deer camps, we boys gathered to sit on the curb and watch the pickups, stake-bed trucks, and cars go by loaded with gear, some pulling horse trailers. There were no four-wheel-drive vehicles before the war and the Jeep. After the war, through your Scout troop, Scouts could buy war-surplus sleeping bags, packs, and pup tents, if you wanted.

By Friday afternoon the traffic became a procession as hunters from Ogden and Salt Lake moved south, some going as far as Kanosh, Richfield, Beaver, and Cedar City. The southern deer were smaller but more numerous, the mountains and ridges not so high and steep. And on Saturday afternoon and evening we gathered again to watch the outfits coming back with their bucks, the antlered heads hung out over the tailgates, our hearts full of envy and regret that we hadn't killed them or at least seen them killed.

Some of the best hunting close to Provo was Strawberry Ridge, Diamond Fork, Birdseye, Hobble Creek, Payson Canyon, Lake Fork, and Tucker. Families and groups of hunters returned to the same camps year after year to hunt the familiar ground. During the war, deer hunters saved their gas coupons to be able to go hunting. Most of the camps housed only men and boys, but some hunters brought their whole families, some camps with two or three families. But the women typically didn't hunt. They stayed in camp to visit, enjoy the campfire, and prepare food.

A lot of hunters who had moved to California to find work in the war industries came back for the Utah deer hunt after the war. We didn't want these hunters killing our deer. But we did like them to drive the bucks up the draws. We thought all California hunters were lazy and dumb; they didn't stand on the tops of the ridges at first light to shoot the big bucks the other hunters drove up to them.

My first deer seasons I didn't carry a gun; I wasn't old enough. I went with Dave and his dad. I helped jump deer. My mother's boyfriend, a man named McBride, took me down to Cove Fort hunting, but he didn't get a shot. We had two flat tires and had to come out on a rim in Mr. McBride's old Plymouth. The first deer hunt on which I carried a rifle, my Scoutmaster, Harold Jones, took me. He loaned me a rifle. We hunted above Indianola. Other members of the party got their buck, but I didn't get a shot. I didn't shoot my first deer until a year later when I joined the army and went to Germany and hunted there.

But even without a rifle, I loved the hunt. I liked to be with men dressed in red hats and sweatshirts, carrying rifles, wearing belts gleaming with cartridges and hunting knives. I liked the smell of sagebrush and sitting around the fire on logs after supper drinking hot chocolate and listening to the stories of previous hunts and how great the hunt would be tomorrow and where the best stands and draws were. I liked sleeping in the big miner's tent with the other men on bales of straw strewn for a mattress.

I longed to fall asleep hearing the howling of wolves, but I knew there were no wolves. You were lucky to hear a coyote. I regretted that the pioneers had killed all the wolves and grizzly bears.

In the morning in the dark we ate fried eggs, bacon, pancakes, and drank more hot chocolate, everybody excited and nervous. Some mornings there was frost and we could see our breath.

We tried to get to the heads of the draws before dawn and waited for the deer being driven up by the hunters below us. Standing on the top of the ridge in the beginning dawn, you waited for the light, kept checking things through your scope, heart pounding, hoping to see a big four-point buck slowly take shape below you in the leafless gray oak brush and maple, raise your rifle to your shoulder and pull down on him, center the crosshairs on his heart. You listened for the first shots from distant ridges, gripped your rifle tighter, hoping you would get a chance too.

I never seemed to be in the right place. I never saw a big four-point working his way up the draw, never watched him turn to look back and then keep coming, never brought my rifle up to aim for a heart or lung shot. But I heard shooting along the ridge and knew that other members of my party were knocking down bucks. Hearing the shooting, you longed to shoot too, were jealous of the other hunters jumping bucks when you weren't.

After the first hour or two, knowing all the pushed deer had come over the top, our party met to start our own drives. Some already had bucks cleaned and hanging in the shade, and they told their stories, the successful hunters laughing and talking, saying how big a spread the buck had, how many points. I was always envious. With their hunting knives they scraped the deer blood out from under their fingernails.

We organized drives, those who had shot their buck dropping down the draw to form a line and push deer out. We gang-hunted, so if you saw three bucks going out, you shot all three, or as many as were needed to fill the tags still left in the camp. Standing on a ledge I longed to see a whole string of bucks go by so I could shoot and shoot, knock buck after buck, but this never happened to me.

If you were near somebody who killed a buck, you went to help clean him, rolled up your sleeves to help split the ribcage and pull out the guts. Finished, you hung up the buck and propped open the body cavity so he'd cool. We washed the blood off our hands with water from canteens or from a nearby spring or creek. But you couldn't get the blood out from under your fingernails, and your hands and arms smelled of deer blood.

When we loaded up to go home, we always hung the bucks' heads out over the end of the pickup bed or trailer or tied the bucks on top of the load so other hunters could see. Driving home we watched to see if other hunters had shot more and bigger bucks than we had.

State Fish and Game had a checking station at the mouth of Diamond Fork where you had to stop for them to see that you had your deer tagged. There was a joke about a California hunter who came through the checking station with a shod mule he'd shot and tagged. The game wardens just told him it was a nice deer and let him go through. There were lots of jokes about California hunters.

I regretted there were no dangerous animals. I hoped that one might have wandered down from Yellowstone Park to make life on the hunt dangerous, or maybe a jaguar come up from Mexico. And I hoped too that a circus train would wreck and the lions, tigers, leopards, and polar bears, their cages broken, would escape into the mountains to hunt the hunters, so you had to be brave. You might see a coyote, black bear, cougar, or bobcat on the deer hunt, but they weren't considered very dangerous. You shot them if you saw them. They weren't protected; there wasn't a season for them.

27

B.Y. High, Mrs. Caine, strapless backless, front teeth

AFTER THE DIXON, Jim Rhodes and I, the only two from our graduating class, went to B.Y. High School, not Provo High. Jim went because his mother insisted. I went because I thought I would get a better education. I was wrong.

I lived across the street from Provo High by then. My uncles and aunts went to Provo High, and all the older boys and girls I knew, and all my friends from Franklin and Dixon. I'd haunted the building as a kid, wandered the halls, sneaked into the gymnasium and auditorium. I knew all the stories about the older teachers. My heritage was Provo High. Everybody went to Provo High. Not going to Provo High was the beginning of perhaps a kind of confusion in my life that was connected somehow with a sense of growing up and facing life, or not facing it.

I walked or rode my bike the nine blocks every day up to B.Y. High on the lower university campus, where I paid twenty-five dollars a year for tuition. Attached to the university as a teacher-training school, it was somewhat exclusive, called by some the sissy school. Many of the students started in kindergarten and came up through the primary grades and junior high school together.

Students hailed mostly from the northeast part of town, their fathers BYU professors, doctors, lawyers, and successful businessmen, not from southwest Provo, where Jim and I were from. I had good teachers, Mrs. Caine, Mrs. Hart, Mr. Tuttle, Coach Crowton, Mr. Snell, Mr. Clinger, and good friends, Owen Heninger, Jim Baird, Clayton McConkie, Cordon Cullimore, George Collard, John Taylor, Don Broadhead. The girls were lovely—Joan Tuttle, Carma de Jong, Audrey Olson, Joan Buckwalter, Elaine Carlson. But it wasn't Provo High, where all my old friends were, kids I'd known and gone to school with ever since the first grade. Without realizing it, I'd come to need them.

Starting as a sophomore, I pledged myself to be a model student and earn only A grades. Within a few weeks, however, Dr. Golden Woolf, the principal, had me in detention for some minor supposed infraction, thus destroying any chance I had of being splendidly exemplary and a light to the academic world.

I didn't earn top grades. But Mrs. Caine, my history teacher, saw that I had potential. She gave six grades for the six units taught during the year. I started out with a C+ and moved upward steadily through B-, B, and so on until I earned an A for the last unit. Mrs. Caine, insightful and fair, the one teacher who sensed my true self, gave me an A for the year.

I had one other academic success. I wrote a poem for Mrs. Hart's English class, which she praised and had me read to the class:

The Snow

The snow falls down in panic flight,
It swirls and turns throughout the night,
But when the morn does softly come,
The snow is gone, its work is done.

Mrs. Hart sometimes wept when she read poetry to the class, urging us to feel the poetry too. I liked English.

B.Y. High was small for a high school, had a student body of a hundred and fifty, all the kids nice for the most part. There were rumors, but I personally didn't know of one boy who smoked or drank beer with any diligence, or fornicated even casually. There wasn't even a rumor of a girl getting pregnant. The lusts of the flesh seemed firmly under control, at least to me. Yet there must have been some moral lapses, at least in the hills above town. Some B.Y. High boys thought it sport in the dead of night to creep up to parked cars on secluded lookouts, open the door, seize the unnecessary garments and run, the darkened hills resounding to curses, screams, and pleas, with sometimes an unclad barefoot lover racing a short painful distance in pursuit and threatening emasculation and even death.

We held dances on the university campus in the Joseph Smith Building ballroom. We took dates, but we had programs and exchanged partners, filling our programs with the names of the couples we would exchange with, and I could watch myself in the wall mirrors gliding by with a variety of girls.

One of the exchanged girls, a senior, wore a strapless, backless evening dress. Still a sophomore, I'd never danced with a girl with a dress like that. I didn't know where to put my hand. I couldn't put my bare hand on her warm, naked back; at least I *thought* it would be warm, had to be. Fortunately, I remembered I had a clean handkerchief in my pocket, as my mother always admonished. I spread this over my hand, and then, properly insulated, put my hand to her back. She thought I was cute and held me close with her long, naked arms.

Another moral dilemma of my conflicted life cropped

up on Friday afternoons, when we had dances in 250-A, a large classroom on the second floor. A tall black-haired girl, another senior, liked to dance with me and would seek me out. She always seemed to wear a long, white, shaggy angora sweater. She liked to hold me close, pushing my face deep into the angora. I had to raise my head to breathe, before she clasped me to herself again. She was tall.

Under these circumstances we boys became very aware of B.O. and used Life Boy soap, which promised the most lasting results. We also used Pepsodent toothpaste because of its promise: "You'll wonder where the yellow went when you brush your teeth with Pepsodent." Yellow teeth would have been a definite disadvantage.

George Collard, who was already, as a sophomore, legendary in his ability to charm women, knew all the right moves — what to whisper, how to hold a girl dancing, how to walk with her down the hall, how to casually and uninvited drop by her house to study, how to put his friendly hand inoffensively on her shoulder. George agreed to teach Jim Rhodes, Jim Baird, and me, three rank amateurs, and pass on his technical skills. But we proved inept, had to admit finally that it took a talent we didn't have and that essentially we lacked charm.

When you were fifteen or sixteen, a Sunday School teacher, usually a sister, giving a lesson on being chaste, might pass around a stick of gum, a rose, or a marshmallow for everybody to hold, and then ask if you would want something that had been handled by other people. It was usually understood that it was a girl that was being handled, not a boy, although why this was so I never learned. I simply assumed that boys, for some strange reason, couldn't be handled.

If the chastity lesson was meant to be particularly

compelling, the teacher would chew the gum, hold it in her hand, and ask if we would want to chew somebody else's gum. The marshmallow and the rose were not chewed. We did not have manuals, illustrated or otherwise, so we could not read up on these important subjects, knew only that adults feared our fertility and its unwedded consequences. I felt unprepared for life.

There were other problems. I was in two plays but never had a lead. I had no athletic ability. I didn't aspire to play varsity sports, but I did at least want to seem adept in my gym class. But I'd never really played basketball, which seemed our primary activity in gym. So that was a disaster. I was still active in Scouting at fifteen, as far as I knew the only boy at B.Y. High who was. And during Scout Week I wore my uniform, my newly earned Eagle badge pinned to my shirt, as we were urged to do to show our loyalty and pride, thus revealing myself as an innocent, even the really nice, not-so-popular girls smiling as they passed me in the hall.

Yet another disgrace came when a bigger, stronger boy leaned forward in my World Civilization class, and, without provocation of any kind, whispered in my ear an insult that questioned my mother's honor. And I failed to stand up, turn around, and knock him flat on his butt with one good punch, which honor required.

The Germans surrendered, President Roosevelt died, we dropped the atomic bombs, the war ended, all the servicemen came home, and there were five thousand people working at Geneva Steel. Shopping uptown, my mother said she never saw a single person she knew. This was also true of the *Herald* obituary page. Because of so many new people, the hunting and fishing weren't as good.

I didn't get my buck my sixteenth year, and the fishing was not going well. I did get to Yellowstone Park with the Scouts and Harold Jones, the Scoutmaster. Mr. Hafen went too, and Bishop and Sister Van Wagenen driving their old Plymouth. Sister Van Wagenen directed all the cooking, which helped a lot, except having a woman on a Scout trip seemed a little strange. Driving around the lake on the narrow road, we saw from the bus window huge trout swimming lazily in the lake, boys leaning halfway out the window in their eagerness. But we had no boat and had to be satisfied with the smaller river trout. Coming home, in Wyoming the fan went through the hood and the radiator, but we salvaged another one out of a dump so it was okay.

I got to fish the Uintas, again with the Scouts, and hooked a magnificent eastern brook trout, the most beautiful trout I'd ever hooked in my life, but I lost him after bringing him in through the rocks three times.

On Rock Creek, Bob Liddiard and I left the other Scouts at our camp, all amateurs, to fish upstream. Returning fishless, we found that every Scout had his limit of one-pound rainbows and bigger. The Fish and Game had dumped a tanker load of planters into the creek fifty feet from camp two or three days before, and nobody had touched them. I considered hanging myself from the nearest pine tree, either that or standing in the middle of the road and waiting for a truck to run over me. My pride, a sin we boys had been weekly warned of in church, had led me to terrible folly.

My mom had fallen in love with a man named McBride, with whom she went for over a year, and when he wrote her a note saying he was going to marry a woman in California, it broke her heart. She cried for six weeks without letup except to sleep.

She cleaned the Clark Clinic, and evenings I would go up to help. Sometimes blood trails led in from the parking lot, up the side cement steps, down the hall, and

into a doctor's office. One night late, Dr. Allen was setting a boy's broken wrist but couldn't put him out, and
he told me to come in and shoot the ether into the gauze
pad over his nose. When that didn't work, he said to
take off the pad and shoot it directly into his nose, which
worked, the click audible as Dr. Allen reset the wrist. The
nurse told me that if I was working late and a drug ad-
dict broke in, I was to give him all the drugs he wanted
and not sacrifice my life unnecessarily.

Because of an infection, I had to have four of my upper front teeth pulled and missed the junior prom.

I worked after school at the *Herald* office, where I was
the janitor, the flyboy who took the papers off the press,
and then the mail clerk. I worked there three years. Bailey Lindstrom, the office manager who wore a white
shirt to work every day, heard me say *damn* once and
said, "Doug, that isn't the kind of language a nice boy
like you should use."

One of the pressmen in the back shop made fun of
me constantly, was cynical and obscene, and tried to
convince me that the world, including me, was rotten,
and I might as well accept that. But if I had a date or had
some other reason for wanting to leave early, he'd tell
me to go and he'd sweep my floors for me. I never did
figure him out.

I went to church, carried out all my priesthood re-
sponsibilities, still aspired somewhat to perfection, tried
to keep all the commandments. I received two Eagle
palms, earning ten more merit badges beyond the Eagle.

My dad had told me once to get an education because
it was the only thing they couldn't take away from you. I
didn't know who "they" were or what other things they
took away, but I wanted to go to college and decided
the only way I could afford it was through the G.I. Bill.

Fearing the government would end the bill, that summer I decided to drop out of high school and enlist.

And I still had my far-off dreams of going to war, although there wasn't one at the time. But still I could be a soldier, volunteer to be a paratrooper and earn fifty dollars a month extra hazard pay, live somewhat gloriously and heroically, come home on furlough with my pants bloused. That winter at a B.Y. High costume dance, every boy but one wore a military uniform borrowed from a discharged uncle or older brother—navy, army, marines, air force, the dream not dead yet.

And so it was time for something new, ultimately time to leave the valleys of the mountains, time for this Mormon boy to go out and dwell among the Babylonians.

About the Author

Douglas Thayer teaches English at Brigham Young University, where he has served as director of composition, chair of creative writing, associate department chair, and associate dean. He has received various awards for his fiction, including the Karl G. Maeser Creative Arts Award. He is the author of the novels *Summer Fire* and *The Conversion of Jeff Williams* and two collections of short stories, *Mr. Wahlquist in Yellowstone* and *Under the Cottonwoods and Other Mormon Stories,* and he has been published in *Colorado Quarterly, Dialogue, Prairie Schooner,* and elsewhere.

Additional Titles from Zarahemla Books

Brother Brigham—In this novel by D. Michael Martindale, C.H. Young has sacrificed his dreams to earn a living for his family—until one day he receives an amazing supernatural visitation. As Brother Brigham's appearances and instructions grow increasingly bold, C.H. struggles to hold together his faith, his marriage, and his sanity.

Hunting Gideon—Jessica Draper's Mormon-flavored cyber-crime novel tracks two crack employees of the FBI's National Infrastructure Protection Center. Through her feline avatar Sekhmet, Sue Anne Jones stalks the V-Net along with her partner, ex-cracker Loren Hunter. Embarking on a wild chase through both virtual and actual reality, they scramble to avert the ultimate online disaster. Draper is the author of Seventh Seal and its sequels.

Kindred Spirits—In this novel by Christopher Kimball Bigelow, Utah-bred Eliza Spainhower has carved out an independent life for herself in Boston. After she makes a love connection with a local native on the subway, she's forced to reckon in new ways with her Mormon identity and her sometimes-overactive religious imagination.

Long After Dark—In these award-winning stories and a new novella, Todd Robert Petersen takes the reader on expeditions to Utah, Arizona, Brazil, Rwanda, and into the souls of twenty-first-century Mormons caught between their humanity, faith, and church. "It is a wonderful book!" says Richard H. Cracroft, emeritus BYU English professor.

On the Road to Heaven—From the author of *Latter Days: A Guided Tour Through Six Billion Years of Mormonism* comes this exuberant and groundbreaking autobiographical novel about the modern Mormon convert experience. Revealing author Coke Newell's hard-won path to meaning, faith, and forgiveness, *On the Road to Heaven* is a love story about a girl and a guy and their search for heaven—a lotta love, a little heaven, and one heck of a ride in between.

Available at ZarahemlaBooks.com

Also available at Amazon.com and other booksellers

CPSIA information can be obtained at www.ICGtesting.com
Printed in the USA
BVOW030335211111

276538BV00004B/4/A